SV

Peter Handke
Versuch über die Müdigkeit

Suhrkamp Verlag

PT
2668
.A5
V47
1989
149365
May 1990

Vierte Auflage 1990
© Suhrkamp Verlag Frankfurt am Main 1989
Alle Rechte vorbehalten
Druck: MZ-Verlagsdruckerei GmbH, Memmingen
Printed in Germany

Versuch über die Müdigkeit

Καὶ ἀναστὰς απὸ τῆς
προσευχῆς ἐλθὼν πρὸς
τοὺς μαθητὰς εὗρεν
κοιμωμένους αὐτοὺς
ἀπὸ τῆς λύπης

Und aufgestanden vom Gebet, kommend zu
den Jüngern, fand er sie eingeschlafen
vor Betrübnis

Lukas 22,45

Früher kannte ich nur Müdigkeiten zum Fürchten.

Wann früher?

In der Kindheit, in der sogenannten Studienzeit, ja noch in den Jahren der frühen Lieben, gerade da. Während einer der Christmetten saß das Kind inmitten der Angehörigen in der dichtbevölkerten, blendhellen, von den bekannten Weihnachtsliedern schallenden Heimatkirche, umgeben von Tuch- und Wachsgeruch, und wurde befallen von der Müdigkeit mit der Wucht eines Leidens.

Was für ein Leiden?

Wie man Krankheiten »häßlich« oder »bösartig« nennt, so war diese Müdigkeit ein häßliches und bösartiges Leiden; welches darin

7

bestand, daß es entstellte, sowohl die Umgebung – die Kirchenbesucher zu einpferchenden Filz- und Lodenpuppen, den Altar samt blinkendem Aufputz in der undeutlichen Ferne zu einer Stätte der Torturen, begleitet von den wirren Ritualen und Formeln der Ausführer – als auch das Müdkranke selber, zu einer Groteskfigur mit Elefantenkopf, auch so schwer, so trockenäugig, so wulsthäutig; entzogen durch die Müdigkeit dem Stoff der Welt, in diesem Fall der Winterwelt, der Schneeluft, der Menschenleere, etwa auf jenen Schlittenfahrten nachts unter den Sternen, wenn die anderen Kinder allmählich in die Häuser verschwunden waren, weit über die Ränder des Dorfes hinaus, allein, begeistert: vollkommen *da*, in der Stille, im Sausen, im Blau des vereisenden Wegs – »es zieht an«, sagte man von solcher wohligen Kälte. Nun aber, dort in der Kirche, die ganz andere Kälteempfindung des von der Müdigkeit als einer Eisernen Jungfrau Umschlossenen, und es, das Kind, ich bettelte mitten in der Mette

heim, was fürs erste einmal bloß »hinaus!«
hieß, und verdarb seinen Angehörigen damit
eine der ohnehin, durch das Schwinden der
Bräuche, immer selteneren Gemeinschafts-
stunden mit den anderen Bewohnern der Gegend (wieder einmal).

Warum beschuldigst du dich (wieder einmal)?

Weil die Müdigkeit von damals selbst schon
verbunden war mit einem Schuldgefühl, von
diesem sogar noch verstärkt wurde, zum aku-
ten Schmerz. Wieder einmal versagst du in
der Gemeinschaft: zusätzlich ein Stahlband
um die Schläfen, zusätzlich ein Blutentzug
vom Herzen; noch Jahrzehnte danach wiederholt eine jähe Scham über jene Müdigkeiten; seltsam nur, daß mir von den Angehörigen später zwar einiges vorgehalten wurde,
nie aber sie . . .

War es dann ähnlich mit den Müdigkeiten der
Studienzeit?

Nein. Kein Schuldgefühl mehr. Die Müdigkeit in den Hörsälen ließ mich mit den Stunden im Gegenteil sogar aufsässig oder aufbegehrend werden. Es war in der Regel weniger die schlechte Luft und das Zusammengezwängtsein der Studentenhunderte als die Nichtteilnahme der Vortragenden an dem Stoff, der doch der ihre sein sollte. Nie wieder habe ich von ihrer Sache so unbeseelte Menschen erlebt wie jene Professoren und Dozenten der Universität; jeder, ja, jeder Bankangestellte, beim Hinblättern der, gar nicht *seiner*, Scheine, alle Straßenteerer in den Hitzeräumen zwischen Sonne oben und Teerkoch unten wirkten beseelter. Wie mit Sägemehl ausgestopfte Würdenträger, deren Stimmen keinmal von dem, was sie besprachen, in ein Schwingen des Staunens (des guten Lehrers selber über seinen Gegenstand), der Begeisterung, der Zuneigung, des Sich-Fragens, der Verehrung, des Zorns, der Empörung, des Selber-nicht-Wissens gebracht wurden, vielmehr unablässig nur leierten, abhakten, skandierten – freilich nicht im Brustton eines Homer, sondern dem der vorweggenommenen Prüfung –, höchstens zwischendurch mit dem Unterton eines Witzelns oder einer hämischen Anspielung für Eingeweihte, während es draußen vor den Fenstern grünte und blaute und dann schon dunkel wurde: bis die Müdigkeit des Hörers in Unwillen, der Unwille in Übelwollen umschlug. Wieder, wie in der Kinderzeit, das »Hinaus! Weg von euch allen hier!« Nur wohin? Heim, wie damals? Dort aber, in der Mietkammer, war jetzt während der Studienzeit eine andere neuartige, im Elternhaus unbekannte Müdigkeit zu befürchten: die Müdigkeit in einem Zimmer, am Rand der Stadt, allein; die »Alleinmüdigkeit«.

Aber was war an der zu fürchten? Stand nicht neben Stuhl und Tisch in der Kammer gleich das Bett?

Das Schlafen als Ausweg kam nicht in Frage: Zunächst einmal wirkte sich jene Art der

Müdigkeit aus in einer Lähmung, aus der heraus in der Regel nicht einmal ein Krümmen des kleinen Fingers, ja kaum ein Wimpernzucken möglich war; selbst das Atmen schien ins Stocken geraten, so daß man sich erstarrt bis ins Innerste fühlte zu einer Müdigkeitssäule; und wenn doch einmal der Schritt ins Bett geschafft wurde, dann kam es, nach einem schnellen, ohnmachtsähnlichen Wegschlafen – keine Empfindung von Schlaf –, beim ersten Umdrehen zum Aufwachen hinein in die Schlaflosigkeit, meist ganze Nächte lang, denn die Müdigkeit im Zimmer allein pflegte immer am späten Nachmittag oder am frühen Abend hereinzubrechen, mit der Dämmerung. Von der Schlaflosigkeit haben andere schon genug erzählt: wie sie am Ende dem Schlaflosen sogar das Weltbild bestimmt, so daß er das Dasein, beim besten Willen, nur noch als Unglück, jedes Handeln als sinnlos, jede Liebe als lächerlich sehen kann. Wie der Schlaflose daliegt bis hinein ins Fahllicht des Morgengrauens, das ihm die

Verdammnis bedeutet, über ihn allein da in seiner Schlaflosigkeitshölle hinaus des ganzen fehlgeratenen, auf den falschen Planeten verschlagenen Menschenwesens ... Auch ich war in der Welt der Schlaflosen (und bin es, immer wieder, noch jetzt). Die ersten Vögel noch in der Finsternis, im Vorfrühling: wie österlich sonst oft – wie hohnvoll aber nun hereinschrillend zum Zellenbett, »wieder-ei-ne-Nacht-ohne-Schlaf«. Das Schlagen der Kirchturmuhren jede Viertelstunde, gut vernehmbar auch die entferntesten, als Ankünder wieder eines üblen Tages. Das Fauchen und Kreischen zweier übereinander herfallender Kater in der Reglosigkeit als das Laut- und Deutlichwerden des Bestialischen im Zentrum unserer Welt. Die angeblichen Lustseufzer oder -schreie einer Frau, in ebenso stehender Luft unvermittelt einsetzend, wie wenn, genau über dem Schädel des Schlaflosen, auf Knopfdruck eine in Serie erzeugte Maschine anspränge, als das plötzliche Fallenlassen unser aller Zuneigungsmasken und das Hervorkehren panischer Selbstsucht (da liebt kein Paar, sondern wieder einmal ein jeder lauthals allein sich) und Gemeinheit. Episodische Stimmungen der Schlaflosigkeit – den beständig Schlaflosen freilich, so verstehe ich jedenfalls deren Erzählungen, können sie endgültig erscheinen, sich fügen zu Gesetzlichkeiten.

Aber du, der doch nicht chronisch Schlaflose: Bist du nun darauf aus, vom Weltbild der Schlaflosigkeit zu erzählen oder dem der Müdigkeit?

Auf dem natürlichen Weg über jenes der Schlaflosigkeit von dem der Müdigkeit, oder, richtiger, in der Mehrzahl: Ich will erzählen von den unterschiedlichen Weltbildern der verschiedenen Müdigkeiten. – Wie zum Fürchten war etwa seinerzeit die Art der Müdigkeit, die sich zusammen mit einer Frau ergeben konnte. Nein, diese Müdigkeit ergab sich nicht, sie ereignete sich, als ein physikalischer Vorgang; als Spaltung. Und sie traf auch nie mich allein, sondern jedesmal zugleich die Frau, so als käme sie, wie ein Wetterumschlag, von außen, aus der Atmosphäre, vom Raum. Da lagen, standen oder saßen wir, gerade noch selbstverständlich zu zweit, und von einem Moment zum andern unwiderruflich getrennt. Ein solcher Moment war immer einer des Erschreckens, manchmal sogar des Entsetzens, wie bei einem Sturz: »Halt! Nein! Nicht!« Aber nichts half; die beiden fielen schon, unaufhaltsam, weg voneinander, ein jeder in seine höchsteigene Müdigkeit, nicht unsere, sondern meine hier und deine dort. Mag sein, daß die Müdigkeit in diesem Fall nur ein anderer Name für Gefühllosigkeit oder Fremdheit war – doch für den Druck, der auf dem Umkreis lastete, war sie das der Sache gemäße Wort. Auch wenn der Ort des Geschehens zum Beispiel ein großes klimatisiertes Kino war: Es wurde heiß und eng. Die Sesselreihen krümmten sich. Die Farben auf der Leinwand wurden schwefelig und bleichten dann aus. Wenn wir einander zufällig berührten, zuckten eines jeden Hände weg von einem widrigen Stromschlag. »Am späten Nachmittag des . . . brach über das Apollo-Kino von . . . aus heiterem Himmel eine katastrophale Müdigkeit herein. Zum Opfer fiel ihr ein junges Paar, das, eben noch Schulter an Schulter, von der Müdigkeitsdruckwelle auseinanderkatapultiert wurde und am Ende des Films, der im übrigen *Von der Liebe* hieß, ohne noch einen Blick oder ein Wort für den andern, für immer getrennte Wege ging.« Ja, solch entzweiende Müdigkeiten schlugen einen jeweils mit Blickunfähigkeit und Stummheit; nicht und nicht hätte ich zu ihr sagen können: »Ich bin deiner müde«, nicht einmal ein einfaches »Müde!« (was, als gemeinsamer Aufschrei, uns vielleicht aus den Einzelhöllen befreit hätte): Solche Müdigkeiten brannten uns das Sprechenkönnen, die Seele, aus. Wären wir dann doch tatsächlich imstande gewesen, getrennte Wege zu gehen!

Nein, jene Müdigkeiten bewirkten, daß die im Innern Entzweiten außen, als Körper, zusammenbleiben mußten. Dabei kam es dann, daß die beiden, von dem Müdteufel besessen, selber zum Fürchten wurden.

Zu fürchten von wem?

Jeweils vom andern. Jene Art Müdigkeit, sprachlos, wie sie bleiben mußte, nötigte zur Gewalt. Diese äußerte sich vielleicht nur im Blick, der das andre entstellte, nicht bloß als einzelne Person, sondern auch als das andere *Geschlecht*: Häßliches und lächerliches Weiber- oder Männer-Geschlecht, mit diesem eingefleischten Frauengang, mit diesen unverbesserlichen Männerposen. Oder die Gewalt ereignete sich versteckt, an etwas Dritten, im wie beiläufigen Erschlagen einer Fliege, im wie zerstreuten Zerrupfen einer Blume. Es geschah auch, daß man sich selber wehtat, indem die eine sich die Fingerkuppen zerbiß, indem der andre in eine Flamme griff;

indem er sich die Faust ins Gesicht schlug, indem sie sich, wie ein Kleinkind, nur ohne dessen Schutzschichten, platt auf die Erde warf. Manchmal fiel ein solcher Müder den mit ihm Mitgefangenen, den Feind oder die Feindin, aber auch leibhaftig an, wollte ihn aus dem Weg schlagen, versuchte sich mit hingestammelten Schmähungen von ihr freizuschreien. Diese Gewalt der Paares-Müdigkeit war immerhin noch der einzige Ausweg aus ihr; denn danach gelang in der Regel wenigstens das Auseinandergehen. Oder die Müdigkeit machte Platz für eine Erschöpfung, in der man endlich wieder Luft kriegte und sich besinnen konnte. Einer kehrte dann vielleicht doch zum andern zurück, und man starrte einander verwundert an, noch durchzittert vom gerade Geschehenen, außerstande, es zu begreifen. Daraus konnte dann wieder ein Anblicken des anderen werden, aber mit ganz neuen Augen: »Was ist uns nur da zugestoßen, im Kino, auf der Straße, auf der Brücke?« (Man fand auch die Stimme wieder, das auszusprechen, unwillkürlich gemeinsam, oder der junge Mann für die junge Frau, oder umgekehrt.) Insofern mochte solch über die zwei Jungen verhängte Müdigkeit sogar eine Verwandlung bedeuten: der unbekümmerten Verliebtheit des Anfangs in den Ernst. Keinem kam es in den Sinn, den andern zu beschuldigen für das, was er gerade getan hatte; es war statt dessen ein gemeinsames Augenaufgehen für eine von den einzelnen Personen unabhängige Bedingtheit in dem Zusammensein, Zusammen»werden«, von Mann und Frau, eine Bedingtheit, die man früher zum Beispiel »eine Auswirkung der Erbsünde« genannt hat, und heutzutage ich weiß nicht wie. Wäre es den beiden gelungen, dieser Müdigkeit zu entkommen, so würden sie in deren Erkenntnis, wie nur je zwei einer Katastrophe Entronnene, hernach zeitlebens – hoffentlich! – zusammengehören, und so eine Müdigkeit würde ihnen nie wieder zustoßen, hoffentlich. Und sie lebten miteinander glücklich und zufrieden, bis etwas anderes – viel weniger rätselhaft, viel weniger zu befürchten, viel weniger zu bestaunen als jene Müdigkeit, zwischen sie träte: das Alltägliche, der Kram, die Gewohnheiten.

Aber gibt es die entzweienden Müdigkeiten denn nur bei Mann und Frau, und nicht ebenso zwischen Freunden?

Nein. Sooft ich in der Gesellschaft eines Freundes eine Müdigkeit spürte, war das überhaupt keine Katastrophe. Ich erlebte sie als den Lauf der Dinge. Wir waren schließlich nur auf Zeit zusammen, und nach dieser Zeit würde jeder wieder seiner Wege gehen, im Bewußtsein der Freundschaft auch nach einer matten Stunde. Die Müdigkeiten unter Freunden waren ungefährlich – die zwischen den jungen, meist auch noch nicht lang miteinander umgehenden Paaren dagegen eine Gefahr. Anders als in der Freundschaft stand in der Liebe – oder wie jenes Voll- und Ganzseinsgefühl nennen? – mit dem Losbrechen der Müdigkeit plötzlich alles auf dem Spiel. Entzauberung; mit einem Schlag schwanden die Linien aus dem Bild des andern; er, sie ergab binnen einer Schrecksekunde kein Bild mehr; das Bild der Sekunde zuvor war bloß eine Luftspiegelung gewesen: So konnte es von einem Moment zum andern zwischen zwei Menschen aus sein – und das am meisten Erschreckende war, daß es dadurch auch mit einem selber aus zu sein schien; man fand sich selber so häßlich, oder, ja: *nichtig* wie den andern, mit dem man doch eben noch spürbar eine Daseinsweise verkörpert hatte (»ein Leib und eine Seele«); man wollte sich, ebenso wie das verdammte Gegenüber, auf der Stelle ab- oder weggeschafft; sogar die Dinge um einen fielen auseinander zu Nichtsnutzigkeiten (»wie müde und verwohnt der Schnellzug vorbeiweht« – Erinnerung an die Gedichtzeile eines Freunds): Jene Paares-Müdigkeiten hatten die Gefahr, auszugreifen als Lebensmüdigkeit, über einen allein hinaus auch des Universums, des schlappen Laubs in den Bäumen, des jäh wie lahm fließenden Flusses, des ausbleichenden Himmels. – Da derartiges aber immer nur geschah, wenn Frau und Mann miteinander allein waren, vermied ich mit den Jahren all die länger-dauernden »Unter-vier-Augen«-Situationen (was auch keine Lösung war, oder eine feige).

Jetzt ist es Zeit für eine ganz andere Frage: Erzählst du von den zu fürchtenden, bös-artigen Müdigkeiten denn nicht nur aus Pflichtbewußtsein – weil sie zu deinem Thema gehören –, und darum auch so, wie mir vorkommt, schwerfällig, langwierig, bei aller Übertreibung – die Geschichte von der gewalttätigen Müdigkeit war doch übertrie-ben, wenn nicht erfunden – halbherzig?

Nicht bloß halbherzig war von den schlim-men Müdigkeiten bisher die Rede, sondern herzlos. (Und das ist kein bloßes Wortspiel, das um seiner selbst willen eine Sache verrät.)

Nur betrachte ich die Herzlosigkeit meines Erzählens in diesem Fall nicht als einen Fehler. (Abgesehen davon ist die Müdigkeit nicht mein Thema, sondern mein Problem – ein Vorwurf, dem ich mich aussetze.) Und ich möchte auch für das Weitere, für die nichtargen, die schöneren und schönsten Müdigkeiten, die mich angestachelt haben zu diesem Versuch, gleich herzlos bleiben: Es soll mir genügen, den Bildern nachzugehen, die ich habe von meinem Problem, mich dann jeweils, wörtlich, ins Bild zu setzen und dieses mit der Sprache, samt seinen Schwingungen und Windungen, zu umzirkeln, möglichst herzlos. Im Bild zu sein (zu sitzen), das genügt mir schon als Gefühl. Wenn ich mir für die Fortsetzung des Versuchs von der Müdigkeit ein Zusätzliches wünschen dürfte, so wäre es eher eine Empfindung: die Empfindung der Sonne und des Frühlingswinds der andalusischen Morgen dieser Märzwochen jetzt draußen in der Steppe vor Linares zwischen den Fingern zu behalten für das Sitzen

dann drinnen im Zimmer, damit diese herr-
liche Empfindung der Finger-Zwischen-
räume, verstärkt noch durch die Duftschwa-
den der Schuttkamillen, übergeht auch auf die
kommenden Sätze rund um die *guten* Müdigkeiten; ihnen gerecht wird und sie vor allem
leichter macht als die vorangegangenen. Aber
ich glaube schon jetzt zu wissen: Die Müdigkeit ist schwer; das Problem der Müdigkeit, in
jeder Spielart, wird schwer bleiben. (In die
Schwaden der wilden Kamille stößt auch immer wieder, und von Morgen zu Morgen
mehr, der allgegenwärtige Aasgeruch; nur
will ich dessen Behecheln wie bisher den dafür
zuständigen, sich bestens davon nährenden
Geiern überlassen.) – Also nun, am neuen
Morgen, auf, weiter, mit mehr Luft und Licht
zwischen den Zeilen, wie es der Sache entspricht, dabei aber stetig nah am Erdboden,
nah beim Schutt zwischen der gelbweißen
Kamille, mithilfe des Gleichmaßes der erleb-
ten Bilder. – Es ist nicht ganz wahr, daß
ich früher nur Müdigkeiten zum Fürchten

kannte. In der Kindheit damals, Ende der vierziger, Anfang der fünfziger Jahre, war das Dreschen des Getreides mit der Maschine noch ein Ereignis. Es wurde nicht automatisch gleich auf den Feldern abgewickelt – zur einen Seite des Automaten die Ähren hinein, zur andern Seite das Herausfallen der mahlfertigen Säcke –, sondern fand daheim in den Scheunen statt, mit einer Leihmaschine, die in der Dreschzeit von Hof zu Hof ging. Für den Vorgang des Korndreschens wurde eine richtige Kette von Handlangern benötigt, von denen einer jeweils die Garbe von dem im Freien stehenden, für die Scheune viel zu großen und zu hoch beladenen Wagen herunterwarf zum nächsten, der die Garbe, möglichst nicht mit der falschen, der ungriffigen, der Ährenseite voran, weiterreichte zur Hauptperson drinnen an der dröhnenden, die ganze Scheune vibrieren lassenden Maschine, wo die Garbe herumgeschwenkt und an den Ährenspitzen sacht zwischen die Dreschzahnrollen geschoben wurde – großes Prasseln, das da jeweils losbrach –, worauf hinten dann das leere Stroh herausgeschlittert kam und, zum Haufen geworden, vom nächsten Handlanger mit einer sehr langen Holzzinkengabel hinaufgehievt wurde zu den letzten in der Kette, meist den vollzähligen Dorfkindern oben im Scheunendachboden, die das Stroh in die hintersten Winkel zu schleppen und in die letzten freien Schlüpfe zu stopfen und festzutreten hatten, je mehr sich davon zwischen ihnen auftürmte, desto mehr schon im Finstern. Das alles dauerte, bis der Wagen vor dem Tor, sein Leichterwerden anzeigend durch ein Lichterwerden in der Scheune, leer war, ohne Pause, in einem rasch ineinandergreifenden Verlauf, den aber ein Fehlgriff sofort ins Stocken oder Schleudern brachte. Auch der letzte in der Kette, gegen Ende der Dreschstunde oft schon eingezwängt, fast ohne Spielraum, zwischen den Strohbergen, konnte, wenn er für das immer noch weiter rasch nachgeschobene Stroh nicht im Handumdrehen noch im Dunkeln neben sich einen

Platz fand, den Ablauf stören, indem er, nah
am Ersticken, von seinem Posten flüchtete.
Aber war das Dreschen wieder einmal glücklich vorbei, die allesübertönende Maschine
– auch keine Verständigung schreiend Mund
an Ohr möglich – abgeschaltet: Was für eine
Stille, nicht nur in der Scheune, sondern im
ganzen Land; was für ein Licht, das, statt zu
blenden, einen nun umfing. Während sich die
Staubschwaden legten, versammelten wir
uns mit wankenden Knien, taumelnd und
torkelnd, das dann auch schon ein wenig im
Spiel, draußen im Hof. Unsere Beine und
Arme waren zerkratzt; Ährengräten steckten
in den Haaren, zwischen Fingern und Zehen.
Das Nachhaltigste aber an diesem Bild sind
unsere Nasenlöcher: vom Staub nicht nur
grau, sondern schwarz, bei den Männern, den
Frauen wie uns Kindern. So saßen wir – in
meiner Erinnerung immer draußen in der
Nachmittagssonne – und genossen redend
oder schweigend die gemeinsame Müdigkeit,
von dieser, die einen auf der Hofbank, die

andern auf der Wagendeichsel, die dritten weiter weg schon im Gras der Bleiche, tatsächlich wie versammelt, in einer episodischen Eintracht, auch aller Nachbarn, auch der Generationen. Eine Wolke von Müdigkeit, eine ätherische Müdigkeit vereinte uns damals (bis sich die nächste Garbenladung ankündigte). Bilder solcher Wir-Müdigkeiten aus der Dorfkindheit habe ich noch mehr.

Verklärt da nicht die Vergangenheit?

Wenn die Vergangenheit so war, daß sie es schafft, zu verklären, so soll sie mir recht sein, und ich glaube solcher Verklärung. Ich weiß, daß diese Zeit eine heilige war.

Aber ist der Gegensatz, den du da nahelegst, zwischen gemeinschaftlichem Handwerk und Alleinarbeit, am Automaten, nicht eine bloße Meinung und also vor allem ungerecht?

Nicht auf so einen Gegensatz kam es mir mit dem Erzählen gerade an, sondern auf das reine Bild; sollte aber, gegen meinen Willen, sich eine Gegensätzlichkeit aufdrängen, so hieße das, es wäre mir kein reines Bild zu erzählen gelungen, und ich muß mich im folgenden noch mehr als bisher hüten, in der Darstellung des Einen dieses stillschweigend gegen ein Anderes auszuspielen – es darzustellen auf Kosten des anderen, wie es das Kennzeichen des Manichäischen – nur das Gute, nur das Böse – ist, welches heutzutage sogar schon im Erzählen vorherrscht, der ursprünglich am meisten von Meinungen freien, weitherzigsten Weise zu reden: Hier erzähle ich euch von den guten Gärtnern, aber nur, um dort um so mehr von den bösen Jägern reden zu können. – Tatsache ist aber, daß ich von den Müdigkeiten der Handwerker herzbewegende, erzählbare Bilder habe, von denen der Automatenbediener dagegen (noch) keine. Damals, in der gemeinsamen Müdigkeit nach dem Korndreschen, sah ich

mich einmal unter so etwas wie einem Volk
sitzen, einem Volk, wie ich es mir später in
meinem Land Österreich immer wieder ge-
wünscht und immer mehr vermißt habe.
Nicht von »ganzer Völker Müdigkeiten«, den
auf den Lidern eines einzelnen, eines Spätge-
borenen, lastenden, spreche ich, sondern von
dem Wunschbild der Müdigkeit des einen,
bestimmten, kleinen Volkes der zweiten
Nachkriegsrepublik: daß all deren Gruppen,
Stände, Bünde, Korps, Domkapitel einmal so
rechtschaffen müde wie wir Dörfler damals
dasäßen, gleich auf gleich in der gemeinsamen Müdigkeit, von ihr geeinigt und vor
allem gereinigt. Ein französischer Freund,
ein Jude, der während der deutschen Besat-
zung versteckt leben mußte, erzählte einmal,
natürlich verklärend, aber um so mehr ein-
leuchtend, nach der Befreiung sei dann
»wochenlang ein Strahlen durch das ganze
Land gegangen«: und so ähnlich wäre auch
meine Vorstellung von einer gemeinsamen
österreichischen Werk-Müdigkeit. Aber: Ein

Übeltäter, ungeschoren davongekommen, nickt zwar oft ein, wo er sitzt oder steht, wie so mancher unstet Flüchtige, schläft dann auch viel, tief und geräuschvoll – nur kennt er keine Müdigkeit, geschweige denn jene, die verbindet; bis zu seinem letzten Röchler wird er durch nichts mehr auf der Welt müde zu kriegen sein, es sei denn durch seine endliche, insgeheim vielleicht sogar von ihm selber herbeigesehnte Bestrafung. Und mein ganzes Land ist durchsetzt von derartigen Unermüd-lichen, Putzmunteren, bis hin zu den soge-nannten Führungskräften; statt je auch nur für einen Augenblick den Zug der Müdigkeit zu bilden, setzt dreist sich in Szene ein wim-melnder Haufen *fortgesetzter* Gewalttäter und Handlanger, ganz andern als den oben be-schriebenen, von alt, doch nicht müde gewor-denen Massenmord-Buben und -Dirndeln, der landesweit eine Nachkommenschaft von gleichermaßen ewig aufgeweckten Kerlchen abgesondert hat, welche dabei sind, auch schon die Enkel zu Spähtrupps zu drillen, so daß in dieser gemeinen Mehrheit für all die Minderheiten nie ein Platz sein wird zu der so nötigen Sammlung in einem Volk der Müdigkeit; in diesem Staat wird ein jeder mit seiner Müdigkeit bis ans Ende der Geschichte dieses Staats mit sich allein bleiben. Das Weltgericht, an das ich einmal, was unser Volk betrifft, tatsächlich einen Moment lang glaubte – ich brauche nicht zu sagen, wann das war –, gibt es dem Anschein nach doch nicht; oder anders: die Erkenntnisse solch eines Weltgerichts traten innerhalb der österreichischen Grenzen nicht in Kraft und werden, so mein Denken nach der kurzen Hoffnung, da auch niemals in Kraft treten. Das Weltgericht gibt es nicht. Unser Volk, mußte ich weiter denken, ist das erste unabänderlich verkommene, das erste unverbesserliche, das erste für alle Zukunft zur Sühne unfähige, umkehrunfähige Volk der Geschichte.

Ist das jetzt nicht eindeutig bloß eine Meinung?

Es ist keine Meinung, sondern ein Bild: denn was ich dachte, sah ich zugleich. Meinung, und damit unrichtig, ist daran vielleicht das Wort »Volk«; denn in dem Bild erschien mir eben kein »Volk«, sondern der verstockte, zur Uneinsichtigkeit seiner entmenschten Taten und zum endlosen Kreisgang verurteilte *»Haufen der Unmüden«*. Aber selbstverständlich widersprechen dem jetzt sofort andere Bilder und verlangen wieder Gerechtigkeit; bloß gehen sie mir nicht so tief, mildern nur. – Die Vorfahren, soweit sie überhaupt zurückzuverfolgen sind, waren Knechte, Keuschler (Kleinstbauern ohne Ländereien) und, wenn sie eine Ausbildung hatten, immer Zimmerleute. Die Zimmerleute in der Gegend waren es auch, die ich wiederholt zusammen als jenes Volk der Müdigkeit sah. Es war damals die Zeit des ersten Bauens nach dem Krieg, und ich als das älteste der Kinder wurde oft von den Frauen des Hauses, der Mutter, der Großmutter, der Schwägerin, mit dem warmen Mittagessen in den Kannen zu den verschiedenen Neubauten im Umkreis geschickt; alle Männer des Hauses, die nicht im Krieg umgekommen waren, auch noch eine Zeitlang der sechzigjährige Großvater, arbeiteten dort mit anderen Zimmerleuten (»Zimmerern«) an den Dachstühlen. In meinem Bild sitzen sie während der Mahlzeit neben dem Rohbau – wieder jenes verschiedentliche Sitzen – auf den zum Teil schon behauenen Balken oder den noch zu bearbeitenden geschälten Stämmen. Sie haben die Hüte abgenommen, und die Stirnen unter den angeklebten Haaren erscheinen milchweiß verglichen mit den dunklen Gesichtern. Alle wirken sie sehnig, schmächtig, dabei feingliedrig und zart; ich kann mich an keinen schmerbäuchigen Zimmermann erinnern. Sie essen gemächlich und schweigsam, selbst der deutsche Stiefvater, der »Hilfszimmermann«, der sich in der Land- und Dorffremde sonst nur durch seine weltstädtische Großmäuligkeit behaupten konnte (Friede sei ihm). Danach bleiben sie noch eine Weile sitzen, leicht müde einander zugekehrt, und unterhalten sich, ohne Witze, ohne Geschimpfe, ohne je die Stimmen zu heben, über ihre Familien, fast ausschließlich diese, oder, wie friedlich, das Wetter – nie über ein Drittes –, eine Unterhaltung, die dann übergeht in die Arbeitseinteilung für den Nachmittag. Obwohl es unter ihnen einen Vorarbeiter gibt, ist mein Eindruck, daß niemand das Sagen, das erste Wort hat; zu ihrer Müdigkeit gehört, daß bei ihnen gleichsam niemand und nichts »herrscht« oder auch nur »vorherrschend« ist. Dabei sind sie mit all den schweren, entzündeten Lidern – ein besonderes Merkmal dieser Müdigkeit – wachen Sinnes; jeder die Geistesgegenwart in Person (»Da!« – Ein Apfel wird geworfen – »Hab ihn schon!«); beseelt (immer wieder das mehrstimmige, unwillkürliche, unvermittelte Anheben des Erzählens: »Vor dem Krieg, als die Mutter noch gelebt hat, haben wir sie einmal im Krankenhaus von St. Veit besucht und sind dann in der Nacht die fünfzig Kilometer durch das

Trixener Tal zu Fuß nach Hause gegangen . . .«). Die Farben und Formen jener Bilder vom fragmentarischen Volk der Müdigkeit sind das Blau der Arbeitshosen, die roten Geraden hingeschnalzt von der Richtschnur an den Balken, die roten und violetten oval-zylindrischen Zimmermannsbleistifte, das Gelb der Zollstöcke, das Oval der Luftblase in der Wasserwaage. Die schweißnassen Haare an den Schläfen sind nun getrocknet und bauschen sich; an den Hüten, wieder aufgesetzt, keine Abzeichen, in den Bändern statt des Gamsbarts der Bleistift. Hätte es damals schon ein Transistorradio gegeben, es wäre, so stelle ich es mir jedenfalls vor, dort von den Baustellen ferngeblieben. Und trotzdem ist mir, als käme aus der Helligkeit der jeweiligen Orte etwas wie eine Musik – die der feinhörigen Müdigkeit selbst. Ja: auch jener Augenschein, wieder weiß ich es, war eine heilige Zeit – Episoden des Heiligen. – Zu diesem müden Volk freilich – anders als zu dem an der Dreschmaschine – gehörte ich nicht dazu und beneidete es. Als ich dann aber später, ein Heranwachsender, einmal hätte dazugehören können, wurde das ganz anders als in der Vorstellung des Essensträgers. Mit dem Tod der Großmutter, dem In-die-Rente-Gehen des Großvaters, dem Aufgeben der Landwirtschaft hörte an dem Hof – nicht nur an diesem einen im Dorf – die große Hausgemeinschaft der Generationen auf, und meine Eltern bauten ein eigenes Haus. Bei diesem Hausbau, bei dem jeder in der Familie, bis auf die Kleinstkinder, irgendwie mittun mußte, wurde ich eingespannt und erfuhr so eine ganz neue Müdigkeit. Die Arbeit, die in den ersten Tagen vor allem darin bestand, eine Schiebtruhe vollbeladen mit Quadern bergauf zu der für Laster unzugänglichen Baustelle zu bringen, auf über den Schlamm gelegten Brettern, erlebte ich nicht mehr als unsere gemeinsame Arbeit, sondern als Schinderei. Die Mühsal des langwierigen, stockenden, vom Morgen bis zum Abend wiederholten Bergaufschiebens traf mich mit solcher Wucht, daß ich keine Augen mehr hatte für irgend etwas um mich herum, nur noch vor mich hinstarren konnte, auf die grauen, scharfkantigen Ziegelbrocken, die auf dem Steg sich wälzenden grauen Zementströme, und vor allem die Übergänge zwischen den einzelnen Brettern, wo ich in der Regel die Karre ein wenig anzuheben oder zu verschieben hatte, um über die Kanten und Kurven zu kommen. Nicht selten kippte die Last da um, und ich mit. In diesen Wochen bekam ich die Ahnung davon, was Fron- oder Sklavenarbeit sein kann. »Ich bin erschlagen«, sagt die Umgangssprache: Ja, ich war am Ende der Tage, nicht nur die Hände wund, sondern auch die Zehen verbrannt von dem zwischen sie gequollenen Zement, in mich zusammengesunken, dahockend (nicht sitzend), erschlagen vor Müdigkeit. Unfähig zu schlucken, brachte ich kein Essen hinunter, und auch sprechen konnte ich nicht. Und das besondere Zeichen dieser Müdigkeit war vielleicht, daß es schien, es

gäbe von ihr keine Erholung. Eingeschlafen
war man zwar fast auf der Stelle, erwachte
aber im nächsten Morgengrauen, kurz vor
Arbeitsbeginn, noch schwerer müde als zuvor; als habe die Schufterei alles aus einem
entfernt, was zu einem noch so kleinen Le-
bensgefühl – Empfindung des Frühlichts,
des Winds an den Schläfen – gehörte, und
zwar für immer; als gäbe es für solches leben-
dig Totsein ab jetzt kein Ende mehr. Hatte
ich vorher bei Unannehmlichkeiten nicht
schnell eine Ausrede gefunden, diese und jene
Schliche gekannt? Nun war ich sogar zu matt,
mich auf die bewährten Weisen – »ich muß
lernen, mich aufs Internat vorbereiten«; »ich
gehe euch in den Wald Pilze suchen« – zu
drücken. Und kein Zuspruch, der etwa auf-
half: Obwohl es doch um meine eigene Sache ging – unser Haus –, ließ von mir keinmal ab die Müdigkeit eines Fremdarbeiters;
Müdigkeit, die vereinzelte. (Es gab im übrigen noch mehr solche Arbeiten, die von der
Gesamtheit gefürchtet wurden, so das Gra-

ben der Wasserleitungsschächte: »Diese Arbeit ist ein Hund, ein Teufel!« Wundersam dann nur, daß mit der Zeit jene Todmüdigkeit doch von einem wich und Platz machte der Zimmerleute-Müdigkeit? Nein, Platz machte einer Sportlichkeit, einem Akkord-Ehrgeiz, begleitet von einer Art Galgenhumor.) –

Eine wieder andere Müdigkeitserfahrung war dann die mit der Schichtarbeit während der Studierzeit, zum Geldverdienen. Man arbeitete da von frühmorgens – um vier stand ich auf für die erste Straßenbahn, ungewaschen, urinierte in der Kammer in ein leeres Marmeladenglas, um die Hausleute nicht zu stören – bis in den frühen Nachmittag oben unter Dach bei künstlichem Licht in der Versandabteilung eines Warenhauses, die Wochen vor Weihnachten und Ostern. Ich riß alte Kartons auseinander und schnitt aus ihnen mit einer mächtigen Messerguillotine große Rechtecke heraus, als Einlagen und Stützen für die neuen Kartons, nebenan verpackt im Fließbandraum (eine Tätigkeit, die mir auf die Dauer, wie früher zu Hause das Holzhacken und -sägen, sogar guttat, indem sie die Gedanken dabei freiließ, durch ihren Rhythmus aber nicht zu sehr). Jene neue Müdigkeit kam nun, sowie wir nach der Schicht hinaus auf die Straßen traten und jeder dann seiner Wege ging. Jäh bekam ich da, allein in meiner Müdigkeit, blinzelnd, bestaubte Brille, verschmutzter offener Hemdkragen, andere Augen für das vertraute Straßenbild. Ich sah mich nicht mehr wie zuvor unterwegs zusammen mit denen, die da unterwegs waren, in die Geschäfte, zum Bahnhof, zu den Kinos, in die Universität. Obwohl ich in einer wachen Müdigkeit dahinging, ohne Schläfrigkeit, ohne Eingeschlossenheit in mich selbst, fand ich mich ausgesperrt von der Gesellschaft, und das war ein unheimlicher Moment; als einziger bewegte ich mich in die Gegenrichtung zu all den andern, hinein in die Verlorenheit. In den Nachmittagshörsälen, die ich danach betrat wie verbotene Räume, konnte ich den Leierstimmen noch weniger zuhören als sonst; was da gesagt wurde, war ja auch nicht für mich bestimmt, der ich nicht einmal so etwas wie ein Gasthörer war. Ich sehnte mich dann Tag für Tag mehr hinein in die müden Grüppchen der Schichtarbeiter oben im Dachboden, und jetzt, im Nachspüren dieses Bildes, erkenne ich, daß ich schon seinerzeit, sehr früh, als Neunzehn-, Zwanzigjähriger, lange, bevor ich mich ernsthaft an mein Schreiben machte, aufhörte, mich unter den Studenten als ein Student zu fühlen, und das war kein angenehmes, eher ein banges Gefühl.

Fällt dir eigentlich auf, daß du Bilder der Müdigkeit, in leicht romantischer Manier, nur von deinen Handwerkern und Keuschlern gibst, nie aber von Bürgern, weder großen noch kleinen?

Ich habe an den Bürgern eben nie jene bildhaften Müdigkeiten erlebt.

Kannst du sie dir nicht wenigstens vorstellen?

Nein. Mir scheint, die Müdigkeit gehört sich für sie nicht; sie erachten sie als eine Art schlechten Benehmens, wie das Barfußgehen. Und sie sind zudem außerstande, ein Bild der Müdigkeit abzugeben; denn ihre Tätigkeiten, die sind nicht so. Höchstens können sie am Ende dann eine Sterbensmüdigkeit zeigen, wie hoffentlich wir alle. Und ebensowenig gelingt mir eine Vorstellung von der Müdigkeit eines Reichen, oder Mächtigen, ausgenommen vielleicht der abgedankten, wie der Könige Ödipus und Lear. Nicht einmal müde Werktätige sehe ich bei Feierabend aus den heutigen vollautomatisierten Betrieben kommen, sondern herrscherlich aufgereckte Leute mit Siegermienen und riesigen Baby-Patschhänden, die am nächsten Spielautomaten um die Ecke ihre lässig-munteren Griffe gleich fortsetzen werden. (Ich weiß, was du jetzt einwendest: »Auch du solltest, bevor du dergleichen sagst, erst richtig müde werden, um das Maß zu bewahren.« *Aber:* ich *muß* manchmal ungerecht werden, habe auch Lust dazu. Und außerdem bin ich, inzwischen im Nachgehen der Bilder, meinem Vorwurf angemessen, ganz schön müde.) – Eine der Schichtarbeiter-Müdigkeit vergleichbare Müdigkeit lernte ich dann kennen, als ich endlich – es war meine einzige Möglichkeit – »schreibenging«, täglich, monatelang. Wieder, wenn ich nachher in die Stadtstraßen kam, sah ich mich als nicht mehr zugehörig zu der großen Zahl da. Doch das begleitende Gefühl war in diesem Fall ein ganz anderes: kein Teilnehmer an dem üblichen Alltag zu sein, machte mir nichts mehr aus; es gab mir im Gegenteil, in meiner Schaffensmüdigkeit, nah an der Erschöpfung, sogar ein rundum wohliges Gefühl: Nicht die Gesellschaft war unzugänglich für mich, sondern ich war es für sie, für jeden. Was gingen mich eure Lustbarkeiten, Feste, Umarmungen an – ich hatte ja die Bäume da, das Gras, die Kinoleinwand, wo Robert Mitchum nur für mich seine unergründliche Miene spielen ließ, die Jukebox, wo Bob Dylan allein für mich sein »Sad-Eyed Lady of the Lowlands« sang, oder Ray Davies sein und mein »I'm Not Like Everybody Else«.

Waren solche Müdigkeiten aber nicht in Gefahr, umzuspringen in Hochmut?

Ja. Ich ertappte mich dann auch immer bei einem kalten, leuteverachtenden Hochmut oder, noch ärger, bei einem herablassenden Mitleid für alle die ordentlichen Berufe, die doch nie im Leben zu einer so königlichen Müdigkeit führen konnten wie der meinen. In diesen Stunden nach dem Schreiben war ich ein Unberührbarer – unberührbar in meinem Sinn, sozusagen thronend, mochte es auch irgendwo im letzten Winkel sein. »Rühr mich nicht an!« Und ließ der Müdstolze sich doch einmal anrühren, so war das wie nicht gewesen. – Eine Müdigkeit als ein Zugänglichwerden, ja als die Erfüllung des Berührtwerdens und selber Berührenkönnens, erlebte ich erst viel später. Das geschah so selten, wie im Leben nur die großen Ereignisse, und ist auch schon lange nicht mehr eingetreten, so als sei es allein in einer bestimmten Epoche des menschlichen Daseins möglich und wiederhole sich danach nur noch in Ausnahmezuständen, einem Krieg, einer Naturkatastrophe oder einer anderen Notzeit. Die paarmal, die mir jene Müdigkeit, welches Zeitwort gehört zu ihr? »beschert wurde«? »zufiel«?, befand ich mich auch tatsächlich in einer persönlichen Notzeit, und traf dabei, zu meinem Glück, auf einen zweiten, der in einer ähnlichen Not war. Und immer war dieses andere eine Frau. Die Notzeit allein genügte nicht; es gehörte auch, damit jene erotische Müdigkeit uns verband, eine gerade bestandene Mühsal dazu. Es scheint eine Regel zu sein, daß Mann und Frau, bevor sie, für

Stunden, so ein Traumpaar werden, beide
erst einmal einen langen beschwerlichen Weg
zurücklegen, sich an einem dritten, ihnen beiden fremden Ort, möglichst fern von jeder
Art Heimat – oder Heimeligkeit – treffen und
zuvor auch noch gemeinsam eine Gefahr oder
auch bloß eine langwierige Wirrnis, mitten im
Feindesland, das auch das eigene sein kann,
bestanden haben müssen. Dann wird es möglich, daß jene Müdigkeit, in dem endlich still
gewordenen Zufluchtsraum, den beiden,
Mann wie Frau, Frau wie Mann, Ruck um
Ruck zueinander hingibt, so selbstverständlich, so innig, wie das, so bilde ich es mir jetzt
ein, in gleichwelchen anderen Vereinigungen,
und wenn auch der Liebe, kein Vergleich ist;
»wie ein Austauschen von Brot und Wein«, so
hat das ein anderer Freund genannt. Oder es
kommt mir, um solch ein Einswerden in der
Müdigkeit zu umschreiben, eine Gedichtzeile
in den Sinn: ». . . Worte der Liebe – ein jedes
lachte . . .«, welche jenem »Ein Leib und eine
Seele« entspricht, auch wenn um die beiden

Körper das Schweigen herrscht; oder ich möchte einfach abwandeln, was, in einem Film von Alfred Hitchcock, die angesäuselt den (noch) eher distanzierten, sehr müden Cary Grant umschlingende Ingrid Bergman sagt: »So lassen Sie doch – ein müder Mann und eine betrunkene Frau, das ergibt doch ein gutes Paar!«: »Ein müder Mann und eine müde Frau, das ergibt doch das schönste Paar.« Oder es zeigt sich das »Mit dir« als einziges Wort, so wie im Spanischen hier das »contigo« . . . Oder in deutscher Form vielleicht statt des: »Ich bin *deiner* –« das: »Ich bin *dir* müde«. Den Don Juan stelle ich mir, nach solchen seltenen Erfahrungen, nicht als einen Verführer, sondern als einen jeweils zur richtigen Stunde, in Gegenwart einer müden Frau, müden, einen *immer*-müden Helden vor, dem so eine jede in den Schoß fällt – ohne ihm allerdings, sind die Mysterien der erotischen Müdigkeit dann vollbracht, je nachzutrauern; denn was mit den beiden Müden war, wird ja für immer gewesen sein, auf

Lebenszeit: nichts Nachhaltigeres kennen solche zwei, als so ineinandergeraten zu sein, und keiner von ihnen bedarf auch der Wiederholung, ja scheut gar davor zurück. Nur: Wie schafft dieser Don Juan seine immer neuen, ihn und die nächste so wunderbar mürbe-machenden Müdigkeiten? Nicht bloß eine oder zwei, sondern tausendunddrei derartiger Gleichzeitigkeiten, die sich, bis zu den kleinsten Hautkuppen, auf Lebzeit in das Körperpaar einschrieben, eine jede Regung wahrhaftig, untrügerisch, ohne einen einzigen Spielzug dazwischen – eben Ruck um Ruck? Unsereiner jedenfalls war nach derlei raren Ekstasen der Müdigkeit verloren für das übliche Körpertum und -getue.

Und was blieb dir danach noch übrig?

Noch größere Müdigkeiten.

Gibt es denn in deinen Augen noch größere Müdigkeiten als die gerade angedeuteten?

49

Vor mehr als zehn Jahren nahm ich ein Nachtflugzeug von Anchorage in Alaska nach New York. Es war ein sehr langwieriger Flug, mit dem Start, lang nach Mitternacht, von der Stadt am Cook Inlet – in den bei Flut die Eisschollen hochaufgerichtet hinein-, aus dem sie bei Ebbe dann, schwarzgrau geworden, wieder hinaus in den Ozean galoppierten –, einer Zwischenlandung im ersten Morgengrauen bei Schneetreiben in Edmonton/ Kanada, einer weiteren Zwischenlandung, mit Kreisen in der Warteschleife, dann Anstehen unten auf der Piste, in der grellen Vormittagssonne von Chicago, der Landung am stickigen Nachmittag weit draußen vor New York. Endlich im Hotel, wollte ich mich sofort schlafenlegen, wie krank – von der Welt abgeschnitten – nach der Nacht ohne Schlaf, Luft und Bewegung. Aber dann sah ich unten die Straßen am Central Park weit von der Frühherbstsonne, in der, wie mir vorkam, festtäglich die Leute sich ergingen, und im Gefühl, im Zimmer jetzt etwas zu versäumen, zog es mich hinaus zu ihnen. Ich setzte mich auf eine Caféterrasse in die Sonne, nah am Getöse und an den Benzinschwaden, noch immer benommen, ja im Innern in ein beängstigendes Wanken gebracht von meiner Übernächtigkeit. Doch dann, ich weiß nicht mehr wie, allmählich?, oder wieder Ruck um Ruck? die Verwandlung. Ich habe einmal gelesen, Schwermütige könnten ihre Krisen überbrücken, indem sie über Nächte und Nächte am Schlafen gehindert würden; die in ein gefährliches Schwanken geratende »Hängebrücke ihres Ich« würde dadurch stabil. Jenes Bild hatte ich vor mir, als nun in mir die Bedrängnis der Müdigkeit Platz machte. Diese Müdigkeit hatte etwas von einem Gesundwerden. Sagte man nicht: »Mit der Müdigkeit kämpfen«? – Dieser Zweikampf war zuende. Die Müdigkeit war jetzt mein Freund. Ich war wieder da, in der Welt, und sogar – nicht etwa, weil es Manhattan war – in ihrer Mitte. Aber es kam dann noch einiges dazu, vieles, und eins eine größere

Lieblichkeit als das andere. Ich tat, weit bis in den Abend hinein, nichts mehr als sitzen und schauen; es war, als bräuchte ich dabei auch nicht einmal atemzuholen. Keine auffälligen wichtigtuerischen Atemübungen oder Yoga-Haltungen: Du sitzt und atmest im Licht der Müdigkeit jetzt beiläufig richtig. Es gingen ständig viele, auf einmal unerhört schöne Frauen vorbei – eine Schönheit, die mir zwischendurch die Augen naß machte –, und sie alle nahmen mich im Vorbeigehen auf: Ich kam in Frage. (Eigenartig, daß vor allem die schönen Frauen diesen Blick der Müdigkeit beachteten, so wie auch noch manch alte Männer und die Kinder.) Aber keine Idee, daß wir, eine von ihnen und ich, darüber hinaus miteinander etwas anfingen; ich wollte nichts von ihnen, es genügte mir, ihnen endlich einmal so zuschauen zu können. Und es war auch wirklich der Blick eines guten Zuschauers, bei einem Spiel, das erst glücken kann, wenn wenigstens ein solcher Zuschauer dabeisitzt. Das Schauen dieses Müden war eine Tätigkeit, es tat etwas, es griff ein: die Akteure des Spiels wurden besser durch es, noch schöner – zum Beispiel, indem sie sich vor solchen Augen mehr Zeit ließen. Dieser langsame Lidschlag ließ sie gelten – brachte sie zu ihrer Geltung. Dem dergestalt Schauenden wurde von der Müdigkeit seinerseits das Ich-Selbst, das ewig Unruhe stiftende, wie durch ein Wunder von ihm weggenommen: alle sonstigen Verzerrungen, Angewohnheiten, Ticks und Sorgenfalten von ihm abgefallen, nichts mehr als die gelösten Augen, endlich auch so unergründlich wie die Robert Mitchums. Und dann: das selbstlose Schauen wurde tätig weit über die schönen Passantinnen hinaus, bezog ein in sein Zentrum der Welt alles, was lebte und sich regte. Die Müdigkeit gliederte – ein Gliedern, das nicht zerstückelte, sondern kenntlich machte – das übliche Gewirr durch sie rhythmisiert zur Wohltat der Form – Form, soweit das Auge reichte – großer Horizont der Müdigkeit.

Auch die Gewaltszenen, die Zusammenstöße, die Schreie als wohltätige Formen im großen Horizont?

Ich erzähle hier von der Müdigkeit im Frieden, in der Zwischenzeit. Und in jenen Stunden war Frieden, auch am Central Park. Und das Erstaunliche ist, daß meine Müdigkeit dort an dem zeitweisen Frieden mitzuwirken schien, indem ihr Blick jeweils schon die Ansätze zu Gesten der Gewalt, des Streits oder auch nur einer unfreundlichen Handlung beschwichtigte? milderte? – entwaffnete, durch ein ganz anderes Mitleid als das verächtliche manchmal der Schaffensmüdigkeit: das Mitgefühl als Verständnis.

Aber was war das Besondere an dem Blick? Was bezeichnete ihn?

Ich sah, spürbar für den andern, mit ihm zugleich seine Sache mit: den Baum, unter dem er gerade ging, das Buch, das er in der

Hand hielt, das Licht, in dem er stand, auch wenn es das künstliche eines Ladens war; den alten Stenz *mit* seinem hellen Anzug *und* seiner Nelke in der Hand; den Reisenden mit seiner Gepäckslast; den Riesen mitsamt seinem unsichtbaren Kind auf den Schultern; mich selbst mitsamt dem aus dem Parkwald wirbelnden Laub; jeden von uns mit dem Himmel zu seinen Häupten.

Und wenn es solch eine Sache nicht gab?

Dann schuf meine Müdigkeit sie, und der andere, der gerade noch im Leeren geirrt war, empfand um sich von einem Augenblick zum nächsten seiner Sache Aura. –
Und weiter: Jene Müdigkeit machte, daß die tausend unzusammenhängenden Abläufe kreuz und quer vor mir sich ordneten über die Form hinaus zu einer Folge; jeder ging in mich ein als der genau da hinpassende Teil einer – wunderbar feingliedrigen, leichtgefügten – Erzählung; und zwar erzählten die

Vorgänge sich selbst, ohne Vermittlung über die Wörter. Dank meiner Müdigkeit wurde die Welt ihre Namen los und groß. Ich habe dazu ein etwas grobes Bild von vier Verhältnisweisen meines Sprach-Ichs zur Welt: In der ersten bin ich stumm, schmerzhaft ausgeschlossen von den Vorgängen – in der zweiten geht das Stimmengewirr, das Gerede, von draußen, auf mein Inneres über, wobei ich aber noch immer gleich stumm, höchstens schreifähig bin – in der dritten kommt endlich Leben in mich, indem es da unwillkürlich, Satz um Satz, zu erzählen anhebt, ein gerichtetes Erzählen, an jemand Bestimmten meist, ein Kind, die Freunde – und in der vierten dann, wie ich es bisher am nachhaltigsten damals in der kläräugigen Müdigkeit erlebte, erzählt die Welt, unter Schweigen, vollkommen wortlos, sich selber, mir wie dem grauhaarigen Zuschauernachbarn da und dem vorbeiwippenden Prachtweib dort; alles friedliche Geschehen war zugleich schon Erzählung und diese, anders als die Kampfhandlungen und Kriege, die erst einen Sänger oder Chronisten brauchten, gliederte sich in meinen müden Augen von selber zum Epos, noch dazu, wie mir da einleuchtete, zum idealen: Die Bilder der flüchtigen Welt rasteten ein, eins und das andere, und nahmen Gestalt an.

Ideal?

Ja, ideal: denn es ging darin alles mit rechten Dingen zu, und es passierten Dinge noch und noch, und von nichts war zu viel da, von nichts zu wenig – alles, wie es sich für ein Epos gehört; sich selbst erzählende Welt als sich selbst erzählende Menschengeschichte, so, wie sie sein könnte. Utopisch? »La utopia no existe«, las ich hier auf einem Plakat, was übersetzt heißt: Den Nicht-Ort gibt es nicht. Bedenk das einmal, und die Weltgeschichte fängt sich zu drehen an. Meine utopische Müdigkeit von damals ergab jedenfalls einen Ort, zumindest den einen. Viel mehr Ortssinn fühlte ich da als je sonst. Es war, als hätte ich, obwohl kaum erst da, den Ortsgeruch angenommen in meiner Müdigkeit, sei da alteingesessen. – Und an diesen Ort reihten sich in den ähnlichen Müdigkeiten der folgenden Jahre noch mehr. Auffällig, daß dabei oft Fremde mich Fremden grüßten, weil ich ihnen bekannt vorkam, oder einfach nur so. In Edinburgh, wo ich, nachdem ich über Stunden »Die sieben Sakramente« von Poussin angeschaut hatte, welche Taufe, Abendmahl und dergleichen endlich einmal im richtigen Abstand zeigten, strahlend müde in einem italienischen Restaurant saß und mich so – Ausnahme, zugehörig dieser Müdigkeit – selbstbewußt bedienen lassen konnte, waren am Schluß alle Kellner einig, mich schon einmal, und zwar jeder an verschiedenen Orten, gesehen zu haben: der eine auf Santorin (wo ich noch nie war), der andere im letzten Sommer, mit einem Schlafsack, am Gardasee – weder Schlafsack stimmte noch See. Im Zug von Zürich nach Biel, nach einer Nacht ohne Schlaf zur Schulendfeier der Kinder, saß mir eine ebenso übernächtigte junge Frau gegenüber, die vom Schlußfest der Tour de Suisse kam, wo sie im Auftrag ihrer da mitmischenden Bank die Fahrer zu betreuen gehabt hatte: Blumen überreichen, Küsse auf die Wange für die jeweils auf dem Podest . . . Es erzählte aus der Müden so übergangslos, als wüßten wir sonst alles voneinander. Einer, der zweimal hintereinander Sieger geworden war und wieder seinen Kuß abbekommen sollte, erkannte sie dabei schon nicht mehr; so sehr, das erzählte sie heiter, voller Achtung, nicht enttäuscht, seien die Fahrer beschäftigt nur mit ihrem Sport. Nun würde sie sich aber nicht schlafenlegen, sondern, hungrig wie sie auch sei, mit ihrer Freundin in Biel mittagessen – wobei mir jetzt ein weiterer Anlaß für jene weltvertrauende Müdigkeit klar wird: ein gewisses Hungerhaben. Die Müdigkeit der Sattheit schafft so etwas nicht. »Wir waren hungrig und müde«, so erzählt die junge Frau in Hammetts »Gläsernem Schlüssel« Ned Beaumont ihren Traum von ihnen beiden: Was sie zusammengebracht hat, auch für das Weitere, waren Hunger und Müdigkeit. – Eine besondere Empfänglichkeit für derartige Müdigkeiten scheinen mir, neben den Kindern – immer wieder das großäugige, erwartungsvolle Sichumdrehen nach dem da Sitzenden – und den Mitmüden, die Idioten und die Tiere zu haben. Ein Idiot vor ein paar Tagen hier im andalusischen Linares, der an der Hand seines Angehörigen abwesend dahinhoppelte, bekam bei meinem Auf-der-Bank-Sitzen nach der Zettelwirtschaft des Vor- und Nachmittags so überraschte Augen, als sähe er da einen seinesgleichen, oder anders: jemand noch Erstaunlicheren. Von dem ganzen Gesicht, nicht nur den Augen des Mongoloiden, wurde ich angestrahlt; er blieb sogar stehen und mußte regelrecht weitergezerrt werden – reines Vergnügen in seinem Antlitz, einfach darüber, daß ein Blick den seinen wahrnahm und gelten ließ. Und das war eine Wiederholung: Dort und dort schon sind die Idioten des Erdkreises, europäische, arabische, japanische, mit kindlicher Freude das Schauspiel ihrer selbst vorführend, in das Blickfeld des Idioten der Müdigkeit einbezogen. – Als ich nach einer Arbeit und einem langen Fußweg durch eine baumlose friulanische Ebene »durchmüdet« an einem Waldsaum bei dem Dorf namens Medea vorbeikam, lagerten dort im Gras ein Entenpaar, ein Reh und ein Hase nebeneinander und führten bei meinem Auftritt, nach den ersten Fluchtbewegungen, ihr Gleichmaß vor, grasrupfend, äsend, herumwatschelnd. – Beim Kloster Poblet in Katalanien begegneten mir auf der Landstraße zwei Hunde, einer groß, einer kleiner, wie Vater und Sohn, die dann mit mir mitgingen, einmal hintennach, einmal mich überholend. Ich war so müde, daß die übliche Hundeangst ausblieb, und außerdem, so stellte ich mir vor, hätte ich durch das viele Gehen in der Gegend schon deren Geruch angenommen und wäre den Hunden vertraut. Diese begannen auch wirklich zu spielen: indem »der Vater« um mich herumlief und »der Sohn«, ihm nach, mir durch die Beine. Ja, dachte ich, das ist ein Bild für die richtige menschliche Müdigkeit: sie öffnet, sie macht durchlässig, sie schafft einen Durchlaß für das Epos aller Wesen, auch dieser Tiere jetzt. – Hier aber ist vielleicht eine Einfügung am Platz: Auf der Schutt- und Kamillensteppe vor Linares, wo ich jeden Tag hinausgehe, wurde ich Zeuge ganz anderer Geschehnisse zwischen Menschen und Tieren als solcher. Davon nur in Stichworten: Die da vereinzelt in der Weite wie zum Ausruhen im Schatten der Trümmer oder Steinblöcke Sitzenden, in Wahrheit aber Lauernden, in Schußweite zu den im Umkreis an biegsamen Stangen in den Schutt gesteckten winzigen Käfigen, kaum Raum für die flatternden, doch um so mehr die Käfige ins Wackeln bringenden Kleinvögel darin, bewegliche Köder für die Großvögel (Schatten des Adlers aber weit weg von den Fallen, bei

mir übers Papier streichend, beim stillen,
auch unheimlichen Eukalyptushain an den
Bleibergwerksruinen, meinem Schreibplatz
im Freien während des ekstatischen Schril-
lens und Posaunens der spanischen Karwo-
che); – oder die wie übermütig mit dem Son-
nenuntergang aus der Zigeunersiedlung auf
die Heide stürzenden Kinder, umtänzelt von
einem grazilen, edelköpfigen Hund, dann,
brüllend, außer sich, als Zuschauer eines
Spektakels, vorgeführt von einem Halber-
wachsenen, bestehend im Aussetzen eines
Hasens auf der Savanne und dem Nachschie-
ßen des Hundes, dem baldigen Eingeholt-
werden des Hakenschlägers, dem Nackenbiß
des Hundes, spielerisch erst, dem Fallengelas-
senwerden des Hasens, seiner neuen Flucht,
seinem, noch rascheren, Gestelltwerden, im
Maul des Hunds Emporgelüpftwerden, so
Hin- und Hergeschleudertwerden, dem mit
der Beute zwischen den Zähnen Über-das-
Feld-Wegrennen des Hundes – langhinsich-
ziehend das Hasengequiek –, Spektakel

schließend mit dem Einzug der Kinderschar
zurück in die Siedlung, der Hund empor-
springend zu des Anführers aufgereckter
Hand, an dieser, an den Löffeln, der Hase
hängend, blutnaß, erschlaffende Pfoten, noch
ein wenig zuckend, seine kleine Gestalt die
vorderste in dem Zug gegen Sonnenunter-
gang, und hoch über den Köpfen der Kinder,
im Profil zu sehen, des Hasen Gesicht, in
seiner Hilflosigkeit und Verlassenheit erha-
ben sowohl über das eines Tiers als auch eines
Menschen; – oder die Halbwüchsigen erst
gestern, auf meinem Heimweg vom Schreiben beim Eukalyptushain in die Stadt: an der
Steinmauer bei den Olivenfeldern, mit Öl-
zweigen und Schilfstöcken, unter Geschrei
vor- und zurückschießend, die Steine ausein-
anderschiebend, und mit den Füßen stoßend,
darunter, jetzt offen in der Sonne, die zusam-
mengerollte, dicke und lange Schlange, erst
einmal außer einem Kopfrucken und dem
Züngeln sich kaum bewegend – noch schwer
vom Winterschlaf? –, das Stockniedersausen

auf sie dann von allen Seiten, splitterndes, aber harttreffendes Schilf, in diesem Geprassel der weiterhin unter Geheul vor- und zurückschießenden Fast-Kinder (in der Erinnerung auch ich dabei), endlich das Sichaufrichten der Schlange, ganz hoch, und zugleich kläglich, nicht angriffsbereit, ja nicht einmal drohend, den Drohhals nur vorführend, als ihre angeborene Schlangengebärde, und so aufgerichtet, im Profil, mit dem verdrückten Kopf und dem Blutaustritt am Maul, auf einmal, im Moment vor dem Niedersinken nun unter den Steinwürfen, dem Hasen gleich, dritte Gestalt, wie die für einen Augenblick in der Tiefe einer Bühne erscheinende gültige, beim Aufgehen eines mit den gewohnten Tier- und Menschengestalten bemalten Vorhangs: — Doch woher in mir bei dem allen dieses Sträuben, dergleichen Schrecknisse, die nichts erzählen, vielmehr höchstens bestätigen, auch noch *weiter*zuerzählen, während, was jene *einenden* Müdigkeiten mir erzählen, in mir ein wie doch natürliches Ausholen,

weiter und weiter – das epische Atmen aus-
löst?

Ja, aber erkennst du nicht, daß das erstere
nicht bloß Schrecknisse waren, und zwar
daran, wie du, obwohl du sie nur registrieren
wolltest, dabei wider Willen fast ins Erzählen
gerietst und dessen Zeitwörterformen, der
Mitvergangenheit, am Ende allein vermiedst
durch Vorsatz – durch einen Trick? Und daß,
außerdem, das Ausmalen der Schrecknisse
anschaulicher, oder jedenfalls suggestiver ist
als die noch so friedsamen Begebenheiten
deiner Epopöe der Müdigkeit?

Ich will aber nicht suggestiv werden. Nicht
überreden möchte ich – auch nicht mit Bildern –, sondern erinnern, jeden an seine
höchsteigene erzählende Müdigkeit. Und
deren Anschaulichkeit kommt schon noch,
zum Abschluß dieses Versuchs, gleich, vielleicht – sofern ich dazu in der Zwischenzeit
müde genug bin.

Was also ist, über deine Anekdoten und Bruchstücke hinaus, das Eine, das Wesen, der letzten Müdigkeit? Wie wirkt sie sich aus? Was läßt sich mit ihr anfangen? Ermöglicht sie dem Müden ein Handeln?

Aber sie ist doch schon selber die bestmögliche Handlung, es braucht mit ihr nicht eigens etwas anzufangen zu sein, weil sie für sich schon ein Anfangen, ein Machen – »den Anfang machen«, sagt die Umgangssprache – ist. Ihr Den-Anfang-Machen ist ein Lehren. Die Müdigkeit gibt Lehren – ist anwendbar. Ein Lehren wessen? fragst du. Früher in der Geschichte des Denkens gab es die Vorstellung von einem Ding »an sich«, inzwischen vorbei, weil das Objekt sich nie an sich zeigen könne, sondern nur im Verein mit mir. Die Müdigkeiten aber, die ich meine, erneuern mir die alte Vorstellung und machen sie dazu sinnfällig. Mehr: Sie geben, mit der Vorstellung, zugleich die Idee. Mehr: In der Idee des Dings berühre ich, gleichsam mit Händen zu fassen, ein Gesetz: So wie das Ding im Augenblick sich zeigt, so *ist* es nicht bloß, so *soll* es auch sein. Und noch mehr: Das Ding erscheint in solch fundamentaler Müdigkeit nie nur für sich, sondern immer zusammen mit anderen, und wenn es auch nur wenige Dinge sein mögen, ist am Ende alles beieinander. »Jetzt bellt auch noch der Hund — alles da!« Und als Schluß: Solche Müdigkeiten wollen geteilt werden.

Warum auf einmal so philosophisch?

Es stimmt — vielleicht bin ich immer noch nicht richtig müde —: In der Stunde der letzten Müdigkeit gibt es keine philosophischen Fragen mehr. Diese Zeit ist zugleich der Raum, dieser Zeitraum ist zugleich die Geschichte. Was ist, *wird* zugleich. Das andere wird zugleich ich. Die zwei Kinder da unter meinen müden Augen, das bin jetzt ich. Und wie die ältere Schwester den kleinen Bruder durch das Lokal schleppt, das ergibt zugleich einen Sinn, und hat einen Wert, und nichts ist wertvoller als das andre – der Regen, der dem Müden auf den Puls fällt, ist gleich wert wie der Anblick der Gehenden jenseits des Flusses –, und es ist so gut wie schön, und es gehört sich so, und so soll es auch weiter sein, und es ist, vor allem, wahr. Wie die Schwester, ich, den Bruder, mich, um die Hüften packt, das ist *wahr*. Und das Relative zeigt sich im müden Blick absolut, und der Teil als das Ganze.

Wo bleibt die Anschauung?

Ich habe für das »Alles in einem« ein Bild: Jene, in der Regel niederländischen, Blumen-Stilleben des siebzehnten Jahrhunderts, wo an den Blüten lebensecht, hier ein Käfer, hier eine Schnecke, dort eine Biene, dort ein Schmetterling sitzt, und obwohl vielleicht keins eine Ahnung von der Gegenwart des andern hat, im Augenblick, in *meinem* Augenblick, alle beieinander.

Kannst du nicht anschaulich zu werden versuchen ohne den Bildungsumweg?

So setz dich, auch du in der Zwischenzeit hoffentlich müde genug, mit mir auf die Steinmauer am Rand des Feldwegs, oder noch besser, weil noch näher dem Erdboden, hock dich mit mir zusammen hin auf den Weg, auf den grasigen Mittelstreifen. Wie doch, mit einem Ruck, so, an diesem farbigen Abglanz, die Weltkarte jenes »Alles beieinander!« sich zu erkennen gibt: Dem Flecken Erde ganz nah sind wir zugleich im richtigen Abstand und sehen die sich aufbäumende Raupe zusammen mit dem wurmlangen, vielgliedrigen, sich in den Sand bohrenden Käfer, diesen zusammen mit der Ameise, die an einer Olive ruckelt, gleichzeitig mit dem Rindenbast, unter unseren Blicken zur Acht gerollt.

Keinen Bildbericht, sondern Erzählung!

Im Staub dieses andalusischen Feldwegs bewegte sich vor ein paar Tagen, so feierlich
langsam wie die Leidens- und Trauerstatuen,
die hier in Andalusien während der Oster-
woche auf Gestellen durch die Straßen getra-
gen werden, das Aas eines Maulwurfs dahin,
unter dem, als ich es umdrehte, ein Zug von
goldglänzenden Aaskäfern ging, und in den
Winterwochen davor hatte ich auf einem
ebensolchen Feldweg, in den Pyrenäen, in
der gleichen Weise niedergehockt wie gerade
wir, den Schnee fallen sehen, in winzigen
körnigen Flocken, im Liegen ununterscheid-
bar von den hellen Sandkörnern, aber im
Schmelzen dann eigentümliche Lachen hin-
terlassend, dunkle Flecken ganz anders als die
von Regentropfen, viel großflächiger, un-
regelmäßiger, im so langsamen Einsickern in
den Staub, und als Kind, in eben dem Abstand zur Erde, in dem wir jetzt hocken, war
ich an einem ebensolchen österreichischen
Feldweg im ersten Frühlicht mit dem Großvater gegangen, barfuß, gleichnah der Erde

und ebenso weltraumfern den vereinzelten Kratern im Staub, den Einschlägen der Sommerregentropfen, meinem ersten, sich immer neu wiederholenlassenden Bild.

Endlich in deinen Gleichnissen des Wirkens der Müdigkeit nicht nur die verkleinerten Maßstäbe der Dinge, sondern auch ein Menschenmaß! Aber warum immer nur du als der Müde, allein?

Meine höchsten Müdigkeiten erschienen mir immer zugleich als die unsrigen. In Dutovlje im Karst standen später nachts die alten Männer an der Theke, und ich war mit ihnen im Krieg gewesen: Die Müdigkeit entwirft am andern, auch wenn ich nichts von ihm weiß, seine Geschichte. – Diese zwei dort, mit den naß zurückgekämmten Haaren, den hageren Gesichtern, den rissigen Nägeln, den frischen Hemden, sind Landarbeiter, labradores, die den ganzen Tag in der Einöde geschuftet haben und einen weiten Weg hatten hierher in die Stadtbar, zu Fuß gekommen, im Unterschied zu allen andern da Stehenden; so wie der eine dort, der allein sein Essen hineinschlingt, hier fremd ist, zur Montagearbeit ins Landrover-Werk von Linares beordert von seiner Wohnsitzfirma, fernweg auch von seiner Familie; so wie der alte Mann, der täglich draußen am Rand der Ölbaumfelder steht, zu seinen Füßen ein kleiner Hund, die Ellbogen in eine Astgabelung gestützt, dort um seine verstorbene Frau trauert. – Dem ideal Müden »wird Phantasie«, nur eine andere als etwa den Schlafenden in der Bibel oder der Odyssee, die Gesichte haben: ohne Gesichte: ihm zeigend, was ist. – Und jetzt bin ich, wenn nicht müde, so doch frech genug, um meine Phantasie der letzten Stufe der Müdigkeiten zu erzählen. Auf dieser Stufe saß der müde Gott, müde und machtlos, in seiner Müdigkeit aber – um einen Ruck müder noch als je ein Menschenmüder – allgegenwärtig, mit einem Blick, der, würde er von den Gesehenen, wo auch immer im Weltgeschehen, sich bewußt gemacht und zugelassen, doch eine Art Macht hätte.

Genug von den Stufen! Sprich doch einmal von der dir vorschwebenden Müdigkeit einfach so, wie es kommt, im Durcheinander.

Danke! Solch ein Durcheinander entspricht jetzt mir und meinem Problem. – Also: Eine Pindarsche Ode auf einen Müden, statt auf einen Sieger! Die Pfingstgesellschaft, wie sie den Geist empfing, stelle ich mir durch die Bank müde vor. Die Inspiration der Müdigkeit sagt weniger, was zu tun ist, als was gelassen werden kann. Müdigkeit: der Engel, der des einen träumenden Königs Finger berührt, während die anderen Könige traumlos weiterschlafen. *Gesunde* Müdigkeit – sie allein schon die Erholung. Ein gewisser Müder als ein anderer Orpheus, um den sich die wildesten Tiere versammeln und endlich mitmüde sein können. Die Müdigkeit gibt den verstreuten Einzelnen den Takt. Philip Marlowe

– noch ein Privatdetektiv – wurde im Lösen
seiner Fälle, je mehr schlaflose Nächte sich
reihten, immer besser und scharfsinniger.
Der müde Odysseus gewann die Liebe der
Nausikaa. Die Müdigkeit verjüngt, so wie du
nie jung warst. Die Müdigkeit als das Mehr
des weniger Ich. Alles wird in ihrer, der Müdigkeit Ruhe erstaunlich – wie erstaunlich
doch der Papierpacken, den der erstaunlich
gemächliche Mann dort unter dem Arm über
die erstaunlich stille Calle Cervantes trägt!
Inbegriff der Müdigkeit: In der Osternacht
einst lagen bei der Auferstehungsfeier die
alten Männer des Dorfs bäuchlings in der
Kirche vor dem Grab, einen roten Brokat-
umhang an der Stelle des blauen Arbeits-
zeugs, die sonnenverbrannte Haut hinten am
Nacken von den lebenslangen Anspannun-
gen in ein Muster von Vielecken ähnlich dem
der Erde gespalten; die sterbende Großmutter, in ihrer stillen Müdigkeit, besänftigte das
ganze Haus und sogar den unverbesserlichen
Jähzorn ihres Mannes; und an allen Abenden

hier in Linares schaute ich dem Müdewerden der vielen Winzigkinder, mitgeführt in die Bars, zu: keine Gier mehr, kein Greifen mehr in den Händen, nur noch ein Spielen. – Und ist es bei dem allen nötig, zu sagen, daß selbst in solchen Tiefenbildern der Müdigkeit die Trennungen bestehen bleiben?

Gut und schön: Eine gewisse Anschaulichkeit ist deinem Problem nicht abzusprechen (auch wenn es die typisch dahingestammelte der Mystiker bleibt). Aber wie sind dergleichen Müdigkeiten nun zu schaffen? Sich künstlich wachhalten? Kontinentalflüge unternehmen? Gewaltmärsche? Eine Herkulesarbeit? Sich probeweise aufs Sterben einlassen? Hast du ein Rezept für deine Utopie? Munterkeitszügler für die ganze Bevölkerung in Tablettenform? Oder als Pulver, beigegeben dem Trinkwasser der Quellenhäuser im Unmüden-Land?

Ich weiß kein Rezept, auch mir selber nicht. Ich weiß bloß: Solche Müdigkeiten sind nicht zu planen; können nicht im voraus das Ziel sein. Aber ich weiß auch, daß sie nie grundlos eintreffen, sondern immer nach einer Beschwernis, im Übergang, in einer Überwindung. – Und nun laß uns aufstehen und weggehen, hinaus, auf die Straßen, unter die Leute, um zu sehen, ob uns vielleicht in der Zwischenzeit dort eine kleine gemeinsame Müdigkeit winkt, und was sie uns heute erzählt.

Aber gehört zu dem richtigen Müdesein, ebenso wie zu dem richtigen Fragen das Aufstehen, nicht das Sitzen? So wie jene alte krumme Frau in dem Gastgarten, wieder einmal weitergetrieben von ihrem auch schon grauhaarigen, doch ewig gehetzten Sohn, sagte: »Ach, *sitzen* wir doch noch!«

Ja, sitzen wir. Aber nicht hier, in der Menschenleere, im Rauschen des Eukalyptus, allein, sondern am Rand der Boulevards und der Avenidas, im Zuschauen, vielleicht mit einer Jukebox in Reichweite.

In ganz Spanien gibt es doch keine Jukebox.

Hier in Linares gibt es eine, eine sehr seltsame.

Erzähl.

Nein. Ein andermal, in einem Versuch über die Jukebox. Vielleicht.

Vor unserem Auf-die-Straße-Gehen nun aber noch ein letztes Bild der Müdigkeit!

Gut. Es ist zugleich mein letztes Bild der Menschheit: versöhnt in ihren allerletzten Augenblicken, in kosmischer Müdigkeit.

Nachtrag:

Jene Kleinvogelkäfige, aufgestellt in der Savanne, sind nicht zum Ködern der Adler da. Ein Mann, der im Abstand neben so einem Geviert saß, antwortete auf meine Frage, er trage sie hinaus auf das Feld, in die Schuttlandschaft, um so im Umkreis das *Singen* zu hören; auch die Olivenzweige, neben die Käfige in den Boden gesteckt, sollten nicht die Adler aus dem Himmel locken, sondern die Zeisige zum *Singen* bringen.

Zweiter Nachtrag:

Oder hüpfen die Zeisige doch für den Adler hoch oben – den die Leute zur Abwechslung *im Sturzflug* sehen möchten?

Linares, Andalusien, März 1989

PARADISE

BY DONALD BARTHELME

PARADISE

DONALD
BARTHELME

G. P. PUTNAM'S SONS/NEW YORK

Published by G. P. Putnam's Sons, 200 Madison Avenue, New York, NY 10016
Published simultaneously in Canada by
General Publishing Co. Limited, Toronto
The text of this book is set in Electra.

Several portions of this novel originally appeared, in somewhat different form, in
The New Yorker. The author is grateful to *The New Yorker* for permission to
reprint. Other sections first appeared in *Esquire,* and gratitude to its editors is ac-
knowledged.
    Line from "I'm Proud to Be a Cow" by Tony Geiss reprinted by permission of
The Children's Television Workshop. Copyright © by Sesame Street, Inc.

Library of Congress Cataloging-in-Publication Data

Barthelme, Donald.
Paradise

I. Title.
PS3552.A76P3 1986   813'.54   86-9424
ISBN 0-399-12921-9

Printed in the United States of America
3   4   5   6   7   8   9   10

TO ELAINE DE KOONING

PARADISE

AFTER the women had gone Simon began dreaming with new intensity. He dreamed that he was a slave on a leper island, required to clean the latrines and pile up dirty-white shell for the roads, wheelbarrow after wheelbarrowful, then rake the shell smooth and jump up and down on it until it was packed solid. The lepers did not allow him to wear shoes, only white athletic socks, and he had a difficult time finding a pair that matched. The head leper, a man who seemed to be named Al, embraced him repeatedly and tried repeatedly to spit in his mouth. He dreamed that his wife, Carol, had driven a large bus, a Metro bus filled with people, into the front of his building. It was not her fault, she told him, a Japanese man who had not had

9

exact change when he got on the bus, in fact had asked her to change a fifty-dollar bill and had, moreover, insisted that she stuff nine fives into little envelopes printed with colorful out-of-register scenes from the Bible for his First Presbyterian contributions over the next nine Sundays, was the true culprit. Simon woke early, five o'clock and six o'clock, cracked new bottles of white wine and smoked tasteless Marlboro Light 100s and wondered what to do next.

He put all the extra beds in one room, the room Anne had had toward the front of the house. Stacked on top of one another they looked like a means test for a princess. He bought a new plant, a gold-flecked acuba, and a pot for it at Conran's, a glazed off-white ceramic number. He cleaned the refrigerator, throwing out seven half-full containers of Dannon Strawberry and Dannon Blueberry as well as four daikon in various stages of reduction. They did love salads. He added the remains of an osso buco, capers and red wine, to his dark roiling sauce base. He found a red wrinkled bra hanging like a cut throat over the shower rail and not knowing what else to do with it, threw that out too. He shifted four thousand dollars from stocks into his Keogh account to help upholster his enfeebled retirement years. He called his wife in Philadelphia but got no answer—still, he'd called. He trimmed his toenails, the monstrous left and the even more frightening right big toes knocked back into civility. He inspected his prick and said, "My you're looking fresh and pretty this morning."

"THIS is so good of you," Dore says, "this is Anne and this is Veronica. This is so good of you. Boy is this place empty."

"I put two of the beds in the back room and one in the front," Simon says, "I thought I'd get some plants maybe tomorrow are you guys hungry let me go see what I've got in the kitchen."

"Booze I hope," Dore says dropping her bags in a corner. "Boy is this place empty. I don't mean that as a criticism."

"The owners left the couch and those two chairs and that's about it. Who would like what? I have beer . . ."

"Beer for me," Veronica says, "where do you sleep, Simon?"

11

"In the middle room. I have vodka, Scotch, white wine . . ."

"Vodka for me," Dore says, "and vodka for my horse here, no that's a joke, Anne will have vodka too. Plants are a good idea. Big plants. Rocks with that, just rocks. Anne will have just rocks too. Really this is so good of you. I guess we figured it a little close in terms of funds—"

"Bloody assholes is what we were," Veronica says. "Believing what they told us."

"So you made a miscalculation," Simon says.

"But this is dumber than necessary don't you think? Dumber than absolutely necessary? Where can I put this?"

She shows him a round thing three feet in diameter, in a canvas case.

"My trampoline. I bounce on it. That's how I keep in shape."

"Anywhere," he says, handing around the drinks, "lean it against the wall. I've got some ribs I can broil you guys eat ribs?"

"God that tastes good," she says, "I was at my wit's end, *we* were at our wits' ends, that jerk at the agency I could kill him—"

"We were dumb," Anne says.

"No point in flagellating ourselves," says Dore, "I drink to Simon. What did you think, Simon? Honestly. When you first walked into the bar."

"I was stunned. Conservatively speaking."

In white lingerie, hand on hip, the three of them,

chatting with the patrons, they'd just finished the show the bartender told him, fashion show every Friday, next week, nightgowns.

"The hell of it is, we gave all this money to Africa. Before we came," Dore says. "That's why we're so low. We each sent three thousand bucks to Africa. To alleviate hunger. We saw this thing on television."

"Probably you can sell the beds after we go," Anne says.

"It's got high ceilings," Veronica says, looking at his Dover White-painted ceilings. "You could hang yourself in here."

Q: You're how tall?

A: Six foot and a bit.

Q: Not much hair.

A: Lucky to have what I've got.

Q: You're not fat. Except for the gut itself. Some few red freckles around the shoulders. One-inch gash in the left lower back, result of falling upon a half-brick in childhood. Slight hemorrhoidal tissue manifested at the flowering of the anus. Wretched-looking toenails.

A: I don't see how you can do this.

Q: What?

A: Practice.

Q: It's not bad. I don't have any special expectations.

A: It would drive me crazy.

14

Q: Ever been subject to epilepsy?

A: I had seizures when I was a child. They stopped. I think it was petit mal.

Q: Scarlet fever?

A: No.

Q: A severe headache every day at approximately eleven-thirty.

A: Sometimes a little earlier.

Q: What do you think about the Knicks?

A: King's knee has got me worried.

Q: Are the women gone?

A: Been gone for a week.

Q: Well I can give you some Extra-Strength Tylenol. That's supposed to be good. You acquired them, maybe that's not the word, in a bar.

A: At five o'clock in the afternoon. The day was quite beautiful. The light, afternoon light—

Q: This bar was where?

A: In a hotel on Lexington. I don't remember the name of the hotel.

Q: What kind of a hotel? Was it seedy, or was it—

A: Seemed to me quite okay. Not a luxury hotel by any means, more of an ordinary tourist place.

Q: You walked into the bar.

A: Which was just off the street. And there were these three women, tall, statuesque even. In a crowd of people. People were sitting at tables and sitting at the bar, and the women were chatting with them. Wearing this marvelous white lingerie. Modeling it. And everyone was being very calm, very cool.

15

Q: You too?

A: I sat at the bar and stared. Discreetly.

Q: Did you order a drink?

A: Of course I ordered a drink. I said to the bartender, What's this? He said, Fashion show. Every Friday.

Q: They'd finished when you came in.

A: The show was over, they were moving about the room chatting with the customers.

Q: Bikini pants burning at eye level.

A: Were you there?

Q: I'm imagining.

A: White merry widows and white teddys and white this and that. It was quite stunning. I couldn't believe it. Two of them were blond, one darkhaired.

Q: Then what?

A: One of them came and sat down next to me. There was an empty seat.

Q: You offered to buy her a drink.

A: She accepted. She wanted a Rob Roy.

Q: What in the name of God is a Rob Roy?

A: Some kind of thing they drink in Denver.

Q: They were from Denver?

A: The Denver area. Two from Denver and one from Fort Lupton, which is nearby.

Q: The white lacy *Büstenhalter* encompassing the golden breasts nudging your arm.

A: She was quite circumspect. Asked me what business I was in. I said I was on a kind of sabbatical.

Q: Which one was this?

16

A: Dore.

Q: Then she gave you the story.

A: It came out piecemeal. About the agency thing blowing up in their faces and how they had no place to stay and no money.

Q: So you said what?

A: I said I had a lot of room but that the place was kind of bare.

Q: And she said?

A: She said that didn't matter.

Q: And you said?

A: I said I didn't know what we were going to do for beds.

"**S**o tell me about Fort Lupton," Simon says to Dore.

"It's between Brighton and Platteville. Basically a wide place in the road," she says. "But pretty wide. We even had crack."

"Did you."

"We had crack very early, before the rest of the country."

"Why was that?"

"Some pioneer cowboy chemists. As a matter of fact I was married to one of them for a while. Guy named Paul."

"Where is he now?"

"In the pen. Got four more years before he can even think about probation."

18

"I'm sorry."

"I'm not. Guy cut me in the face one time with a linoleum knife. He was explaining himself."

Simon doesn't understand how anybody could do this. "What was he mad about?"

"He'd been fired a lot, from various jobs. Usually he got fired the first week. He was good at getting hired but he was a genius at getting fired. I was in a shelter for battered women for six weeks. They didn't let anybody know where it was."

"All of you been married?"

"Not Anne. She's never found the right guy."

"Your husband was the right guy?"

"Well he seemed nice in the beginning, Simon. He gave me an off-the-road vehicle for a wedding present. Those are big in Colorado."

Veronica is fiddling with a shirt button. They're in the sitting room.

"What was your first sexual experience, Simon?"

He thinks for a moment. "I was about ten. This teacher asked us all to make little churches for a display, kind of a model of a church. I made one out of cardboard, worked very hard on it, and took it in to her on a Friday morning, and she was pleased with it. It had a red roof, colored with red crayon. Then another guy, Billy something-or-other, brought in one that was made of wood. His was better than mine. So she tossed mine out and used his."

"That was your first sexual experience?"

"How far back do you want to go?"

"How old's your kid? Sarah, is it Sarah?"

19

"Sarah. She's nineteen. When she was little she used to sing 'I'm proud, proud, proud to be a cow.' That's something the cows sing on *Sesame Street*."

"Do you miss her?"

"Of course."

"What does your wife want?"

"More fun."

"What's the matter with that?"

"Not a thing in the world."

"What does she do?"

"She's a lawyer in Philadelphia. A deputy mayor, at the moment."

"You straight or gay?"

"Historically, straight."

"Me too. Nothing wrong with being straight."

"Right."

"Great twat out there on the streets you want some of it?"

"Only in principle."

"You like young twat, go after it. Onward to the merry hunt. You ever live and love in a garage apartment?"

"Never have."

"They're kind of snug. Especially if it's a three-car garage. Up in the trees."

"Must be nice."

"Depends upon who you're cohabiting with. Dore has a hatpin. Six inches of cold steel."

"To discourage creeps and weirdos."

"You got it."

"Has she stuck anybody with it?"

"Not in New York State. I've been reading in the paper about these rabid skunks."

"They're getting closer."

"You wouldn't think you'd have to worry about them in a city like this."

"It's a great city. We have everything."

"The mayor seems like a clown."

"He's a great mayor. He's got it down exactly right. Couldn't be better. He's what we want."

There's a funny chirping noise. It's the smoke alarm.

"What the fuck is that?"

"The smoke alarm."

"What's it trying to say? There's no smoke."

"Telling us that the battery's wearing down."

"Well disconnect it for Christ's sake."

He does so, standing on a chair, my God how cheap can plastic be? feels like paper—

"You've got a good ass Simon."

The *Times* is spread all over the bar in the kitchen.

"This one I like," Simon says. "Death May Haunt Calcutta's Streets, But Teeming City Throbs With Life."

"Unbeatable," says Anne. She's making a salad.

"Although—"

"What?"

"Slain U.S. Major Had One Exploit."

"A one-exploit man."

"Rather like having only one—"

"That was lousy Tex-Mex last night."

"Better than no Tex-Mex at all."

"True."

"What's that weed you're putting in there?"

"That's Venetian marigold. Tastes like mint."

"Oh. Looks funny."

"It does, it does."

She's slicing a big radish with rapid Japanese strokes.

"Anyone who sees *Parsifal* twice is a blithering idiot."

"You mean the movie."

"In any form. Land, sea, or in the air."

"Well I won't take you. You have my word."

"Thanks. This salad is going to be good. I guarantee it. Let me have the lemon-pepper."

"Here. You using the fancy olive oil?"

"Extra-virgin. Just like me."

SIX o'clock in the morning. He's awakened by voices from the back of the house, from outside. A woman laughing.

He gets out of bed and walks to the big second-floor windows overlooking the garden below.

In the next garden, separated from the one beneath him by a high wooden fence, a man and a woman are stretched out on the flagstones, making love. The fence slashes them in half diagonally. The woman lies on top of the man, her dark-red skirt bunched about her hips. Simon can't see the color of her hair.

He rubs his eyes and goes to the refrigerator. Reaches for a bottle of white wine which sits, corkless, in the re-frigerator door. He pours wine into a tumbler, tastes it,

makes a face, and walks back into the bedroom for his
cigarettes.

Behind him the man's voice says "Hey, hey, hey."

Six o'clock? And the flagstones can't be wonderfully
comfortable. Ardent lovers must these lovers be.

The building he's living in is one hundred and seven
years old. The window wall in the back has separated
from the party wall and light can be seen between
them.

Simon, early in the morning, stuffs spackle into the
opening, and, two hours later, sloshes a little white
paint over it. Not bad for government work, he thinks.

The big closet has a large jagged hole in the ceiling,
little tufts of insulation floating at its edges. He decides
to do nothing about this; he won't be here forever. He's
been told not to use either of the fireplaces because the
chimneys have not been cleaned for years.

He closes up his paint can and washes out his brush.
Now, breakfast. Popovers from the deli with rare
cheeses.

On his way out to the deli to get the group breakfast
he hears giggling from the front room. Did you sleep
well? And you? And you? Outside, on the street, someone's screaming.

Peering from the front window he sees two men
beating a cop with a nightstick and fists. The cop is a
black woman, slight of build. There's blood on the
back of her head. Simon throws open the window and
yells *"Hey!"* —a prodigious shout, the shout that kills.
The astonished men look around, then take off in two

different directions. Simon runs out the door and rushes down the stairs.

The cop is trying to pull herself to her feet by the iron railing in front of the building and at the same time wiping blood from the scalp wound out of her eyes. Simon places his hands under her arms, half-drags her to the steps, sits her down.

"Motherfuckers," she says. "Goddamn mother-fuckers."

"Sit still," he says. "I'll call an ambulance."

"Don't need no ambulance. Where's my stick?"

Simon retrieves it for her. She's produced a handkerchief and is holding it to her head.

"Where's my cap?"

He finds the uniform cap and hands it to her. She stuffs the handkerchief inside the cap and places it on her head. She leans forward, half-rises, then moans and sits down again.

"Motherfuckers."

"You want me to call the precinct?"

"No. I'll be fine. Just gimme a minute."

She's pretty, maybe twenty-eight or twenty-nine.

"Those creeps had more muscle than I figured them for," she says. "Perps lookin' for something to make happen. Shake 'em down and you'll find burglar tools. They dress up all raggedy and you think they're not as young as they really are. Got my damn stick away from me."

"You want me to walk you down to the hospital?"

"I'm gonna walk in just a minute."

She pulls a radio from her back pocket and calls in, telling the precinct about "two white males, lookin' to do a break-in," and the location.

"Thank you," she says to Simon. "You're a good citizen. Got a good yell on you." She stands and, staggering slightly, moves off down the street. She turns and calls again, "Thank you!"

Simon goes back inside and pours another glass of wine. Death may haunt Calcutta's streets, but teeming city throbs with life.

Q: You got the beds.

A: I went to this bed store and bought three beds. The guy said for an extra fifty he could deliver them by eight o'clock. He had his own truck, he said. Got them there right on the button. We stripped off the cardboard and plastic and set them up. Two in the back room and one in the little room in the front.

Q: Where were you?

A: I had the bedroom in the middle. I already had a bed.

Q: You'd sublet this place.

A: For a year. The owners had left me the bare essentials, dishes, towels, that sort of thing. A few pieces of furniture.

27

Donald Barthelme

Q: Did the women like it?

A: They kept saying, This is so good of you. The other thing they said was, Probably you can sell the beds after we go. They'd sent all their money to Africa. To fight hunger.

Q: Did they just hang around all day, or what?

A: They came and went. They enjoyed the city. They went to Bloomingdale's and the Met. They went to the Cloisters. They went to Asti's and banged on their water glasses while the Anvil Chorus was being sung. They went to Sweet Basil and heard Wynton Marsalis. I went with them that night, he played very well, had his brother Branford on tenor. They went to the Museum of Modern Art and bought postcards in the gift shop. They went to Lincoln Center and saw various things, the film festival and all that. They got excited by the Strand and came back with books. They went to the Palladium and saw Lily Tomlin or somebody. They didn't always go together. Sometimes Veronica and Dore went, sometimes Anne went by herself, and so on. Sometimes they went together to Balducci's and came home with various exotic foods. They cooked together, sometimes. I remember a particularly good Cream of Four Onion soup. They spent a lot of time just walking around looking at things. I think they were happy. Although in limbo.

Q: Limbo.

A: They were in an in-between state, it was hard on them. I'd come in and Anne would be sitting on the couch, weeping. The couch wasn't much. Some kind of

28

dull gray fabric. Ask her why she's weeping and she'd say she didn't know. Veronica hit me once. Hauled off and slugged me in the chest. It was just frustration. Still, I wondered what in her gave her permission to slug me. Then she made a pie, a blueberry pie—

Q: Did they ever go to Fizz?

A: I believe they went there quite often.

Q: What went on there?

A: It was a meat rack, a heterosexual meat rack. From what they've told me.

Q: So they picked up guys there . . .

A: They did, I suppose. They may have been just playing, just exercising . . .

Q: How did that make you feel?

A: I didn't like it.

Q: Sometimes I think I should have been a shrink.

A: Why aren't you?

Q: It's not medicine.

A: I imagine them thinking, talking to each other . . .

Q: What did they say to each other?

A: I don't know, of course. I imagine they were careful, thoughtful. Direct.

Q: My wife was the world's champion at leaving things lying around. I spent much of my marriage picking up after her. She'd *strew* things about, as a sower scatters seed over a field. She could not so much as strike a match without leaving the matchbook and a burnt match on some convenient surface. If she'd go into the john with a magazine you could be sure that she'd leave the magazine in the john, open to the page

29

she'd been reading. She was a marvel. You'd call this to her attention and she wouldn't understand what you were talking about. Little balls of Kleenex everywhere, yellow Kleenex, occasional grapefruit hulls— Were you worried that it would end?

A: Good Lord no. Maybe worried that it wouldn't. Those women were powerful presences. Took up a lot of space, made a lot of clatter. There were days when I couldn't hear myself think.

Q: All in all, then, it was on the stressful side.

A: We talked a lot. I think of it as a series of conversations. A series of ordinary conversations. Simple as pie. They were very good people. I miss them.

Q: Do you hear from them?

A: Postcards.

Q: These women spread out before you like lotus blossoms. . . .

A: Not exactly like lotus blossoms.

Q: Open, blooming. . . .

A: More like anthills. Splendid, stinging anthills.

Q: You fall face down onto an anthill.

A: Something like that.

Q: The ants are plunging toothpicks into your scrotum, as it were. As they withdraw the toothpicks, little particles of flesh like shreds of ground beef adhere to the toothpicks.

A: Very much like that. How did you know?

Q: I'm not inexperienced.

A: By what standard?

Q: Generally accepted standards.

Sunday morning. Simon listening to one of his radios.

"Jesus is a rock in a weary land," says the radio. The preacher is black, with a deep sonorous voice.

"I wrote a little song that says, don't wait till the battle is over, you can shout now. 'Cause you know that in the end, you gonna be victorious. That don't mean you ain't gonna cry. That don't mean you ain't gonna feel pain. But in the end, you will prevail, in His name. Lift your face to Him, and let Him lead the way. Rejoice. It's all right. Rejoice. It's all right. Rejoice. It's alllllllright. Despite what may be going on around you, you *can*, you *can* find perfect peace. How much, continuously, do we love Him."

Simon thinks about a day many years before when his wife was taking the baby to the park. "Goodbye, you dirty rat," his wife said. The baby was wearing a blue parka and a brown knitted watch cap. "Goodbye, you dirty rat," the baby said.

When Sarah was born he stood in the delivery room wearing green paper pants, a green paper shirt, paper bags on his feet and a green paper cap on his head. He lacked only a fool-yellow rubber bulb of a nose to be a perfect clown.

He pressed his back against the green-painted wall, trying to keep out of the way. His wife had been in labor two hours and forty minutes; a monitor had indicated fetal distress and the doctor, a man known for not doing Caesareans, had a choice to make. The doctor's name was Zernikie and he had a pair of large dull-steel forceps inside the birth canal and was grappling for purchase. The instrument looked to Simon, who knew something of the weight and force of tools, capable of shattering the baby's head in an instant. After all these years, he thought, that's the best they can do?

Carol was gripping his hand. The doctor glanced at Simon and said, "Gross, isn't it?" The circulating nurses exchanged pained looks.

"No no," he had said, "doing fine, keep going."

Zernikie had run eighteen blocks in a blizzard to get to the hospital after discovering that his car wouldn't start. He took hold of the head with the forceps and pulled, calmly and steadily. The head, bright with blood, emerged to the level of the eyes. The doctor rotated the shoulders, pulled the baby out and placed it on the mother's stomach. A nurse began sponging the baby's face as the doctor cut and tied off the cord. The baby had dark bruises on either side of her head. A nurse picked her up. "Here's Sarah," she said. Simon said, "Hello, Sarah."

WHEN he found a pipe bomb wired under his Volvo Simon left Philadelphia. He'd been working on transforming an old armory in a rundown area into a school and had just ordered the contractor to rip out and replace six thousand square feet of expensive casement windows. Probably the man's profit on the job, he figured. On the other hand, the bomb might have come from any one of a half-dozen small suppliers who were not allowed to bid the project because they couldn't make a performance bond. Or, he told himself, it could have been the ghost of Louis Kahn, mad with jealousy. The Volvo had been leaking oil and he'd gotten into the habit of bending down to check the pavement for oil traces after he'd been parked for any length of time.

The bomb was tied neatly to the tailpipe. The bomb squad came, big burly men in aprons like goalies wear with the difference that these were made of Kevlar. They had a barrel-shaped truck draped in wire mesh. "An extremely well-done bomb," a sergeant told him, after the device was safely in the truck. Simon had turned the job over to one of his partners and given himself a sabbatical, his first in fourteen years. In reality, it wasn't the bomb but the prospect of listening to his wife's voice for another hour, another minute.

When she was a child Sarah would occasionally stick a 9D battery in Simon's ear and he would then make a sound like a fire engine, or, alternately, a garbage truck. When the women were living with him Simon and one or another of them would sometimes go together to the A & P, at the appropriate hour, just to watch the firemen buy supper for the firehouse. The double-jointed engine was double-parked outside the store with a fireman in the cab, waiting, and inside four or five tall healthy young men in dark blue FDNY t-shirts would be arguing about what to put in the spaghetti sauce. "I'm up to here with mushrooms," Shorty would say, fiercely, and another guy would lobby for hot Italian sausage. The firemen were good-looking, Simon noticed, appeared strong and trustworthy and very decent. He wondered about the fireman-population, where all this decency and goodness came from. The firemen gazed at Veronica or Dore and then looked away, abashed. Later Veronica, or Dore, would say, "Don't

35

be jealous, Simon." Then, after a pause, "We're not harpies." Did she mean that the firemen were too young or rather in some sense sacrosanct? He had given Sarah a fire engine she could sit in when she was four and she had put out many exciting fires with it.

Bridges should not be painted blue, Simon thought, the horrible Izod blue of the Ben Franklin bridge in Philadelphia ever in his mind. Concrete, he felt, wonderfully useful and wonderfully ugly, should never be seen in public unless covered with ivy, or, better still, wallpaper. Steel was pretty, he did not know why. Brick was good and wood best, for all purposes under the sun. As a student he had submitted a project to redo Rockefeller Center in pickled pine. He had also, on formal occasions, worn a dog collar instead of a tie, most *sportif.*

He'd dreamed that he was supposed to be on television for five hours and had prepared nothing. The television people, young men with clipboards, were friendly, were standing around waiting for him to get dressed and proceed to the studio. They seemed confident that he could do what he had contracted to do. There were some notes in another building, a building far from the building in which he was getting dressed, which might help him if he could reach them in time. His gray pin-striped coat was binding his arms like a straitjacket and Simon struggled against it as the clock indicated that time was passing. When he had missed the opening of the program—he had removed and replaced the jacket several times, each time with enor-

mous exertion—the television people became un-
friendly and began making supercilious remarks. He
had the sense that he could still salvage the situation if
he could get to the building where his notes rested in a
manila folder. Yes, he'd be late, but the notes were of
value, incomplete to be sure but enough to allow him
to bullshit his way through the performance, the second, third, fourth, and fifth hours, or, now, the third,
fourth, and fifth hours, because time was passing and
he had, somehow, put on his blue Oxford shirt over the
gray pin-striped jacket, which was, he understood,
wrong—

"SIMON, you're famous!" Veronica says. She's waving a copy of *Progressive Architecture*.

"You saw the piece."

"Looks beautiful. Big building."

"Four million something."

"It's got a very fancy outside."

"Some of that's fiberglass. We had to take molds to reproduce a lot of the capitals, that stuff on top of the columns. It drives you crazy because you've got to add a fire-retardant to the gel coat and that can change the color and you're trying to match the color of the existing building."

"Do architects make a lot of money?"

"You can go broke," he says. "You can do very well.

38

The more time you put into a job, the less money you make. My partners kept me solvent."

"What's it feel like to be famous?"

"Feels very much like not being famous."

"Are you going to fall in love with one of us?"

She's serious.

"How could I not?"

"It could all come to nothing," she says.

They're in the back of the house, sitting at the bar in the kitchen, looking out of the windows. It's getting warmer, Simon thinks.

"You're what, fifty-three?"

"Yes."

"That's pretty old."

"And life is short."

"When I was in high school," Veronica says, "they dedicated the yearbook every year to the guys from our school who had been killed in Vietnam. They had pictures, every year, of the latest bunch. Every year for four years. So you're married, huh?"

"Yes. More or less."

"I was married. Wasn't so bad, wasn't so great. We used to screw every morning before he went to work."

"Every damn morning?"

"Well not *every* morning Simon don't be so literal-minded."

"In the morning I got the clenched jaw," Simon says. "I knew that something had happened the night before."

"Like what?"

"A fight."

"You couldn't remember?"

"I was drinking. I cooked a lot in the evening and when I cooked I drank. Mingling two pleasures."

"Are you a good cook?"

"Getting there. Give me another ten years."

"Look! In the sky!"

A silver blimp, then another, like two silver buildings majestically horizontal.

"When I got married," she says, "I married this guy who was a Catholic. So we had to get a priest to do the job. So I called this priest and explained the situation. I said I was not a Catholic. And the priest says, 'Well, we can work with you on that.' Then I told him I was still married to another guy, the guy I was married to before I met this guy. And the priest says, 'Well, we can work with you on that.' So I just thought I'd tell him that I was born without a vagina, that I just had this sort of marble insert where the vagina was supposed to be, to see if he would say, 'Well, we can work with you on that.'"

SIMON is amazed by what he doesn't care about. He's bought nothing but a couple of new shirts and a few books. He's thought of no new projects. He reads *Progressive Architecture* and critiques what he sees there in a mood of amiable colleagueship. He'd done a building in 1981 that had pleased him, a Catholic church in a not-good area near Temple University, where the liquor stores gave you your bottle by request over a formidable counter, no browsing in the stacks. The parish was so poor that he'd cut his fee to almost nothing; the other partners were not happy about it but had accommodated him. The church was a bare-bones steel building with insets of glass block as its only design flourish, these however stacked eighteen feet high

41

in twelve bays on either side of the sanctuary—the glass block was the light-giving element, and resisted thievery, too. It had been popular in the 30s, considered a design cliché in the 40s, 50s, 60s and 70s, and presented itself again in the 80s, fresh as new dung. Something to be said for being fifty-three, you could enjoy the turning of the wheel. He feels every additional day a great boon. He doesn't understand people who have futures, palpable futures. He takes an interest in the obituary pages of the newspapers, the summations, tidy packages, So-and-so gets three inches whereas Tra-la-la got seven. He has a pain where his liver is presumed to be and is vomiting rather too much. He's paid $35,107 in Federal taxes for last year and has before him a request from the IRS for an additional $41.09. These people are wonderful, he thinks, they want the last forty-one bucks and nine cents. You'd think with the thirty-five thou they'd say let's have a beer and forget about it.

Dore is brusque upon awakening, Anne cheerful as a zinnia. Veronica frequently comes to the breakfast table (hardly a table, a slab of butcher block on top of some cabinets with four stools around it) pale with despair, then is overtaken with great gusts of enthusiasm, for *Lohengrin* or oyster mushrooms or Pierre Trudeau. They're so lovely that his head whips around when one of them enters the room, exactly in the way one notices a strange woman in a crowd and can't avoid, can't physically avoid, loud and outrageous staring. My senses are being systematically dérégled, he thinks, forgive me,

Rimbaud. Dore is relatively tall, Anne not so tall (but they are all tall), Veronica again the middle term. Breasts waver and dip and sway from side to side under t-shirts with messages so much of the moment that Simon doesn't understand a tenth of them: ALLY SHEEDY LIVES! Who is Ally Sheedy? In what sense does she live, and why is the fact worthy of comment? They know, he doesn't. Simon has actually met Pierre Trudeau (at a three-day city-planning conference in Ottawa) and found him a charming and thoughtful man. This earns him about a crayon's worth of credit with his guests.

He attempts generalizations. Dore is *crusty*, Veronica is *volatile*, Anne is *a worrier*. The generalizations are banal but comforting, like others he's been faithful to over many years, architecture is *frozen music* and art is *a source of life*.

In the middle of the night he senses someone standing over his bed.

"Who's that?"

"It's me. Dore."

He switches on the bedside lamp.

"What's up?"

"Do you have any money?"

"You mean cash? In the house?"

"I need a couple of hundred."

"Right now?"

She's wearing a white lace peignoir with long filigree sleeves.

"Right now. Two hundred, if you have it."

"Let me look."

Simon gets out of bed and opens a book, *On Adam's House in Paradise*. He takes out a stack of bills and counts out two hundred in twenties.

"It's my bad brother," Dore says. "He's downstairs. He always arrives without warning. One of his endearing traits. Thanks. I'll pay you back."

She gives him a quick kiss and starts to leave, then pauses.

"What's your wife's name, Simon?"

"What's my wife's name?"

"You don't have to tell me."

"Carol."

"Pretty name."

They say, repeatedly:

"See what I'm saying?"

"See what I'm saying?"

"See what I'm saying?"

A: In the dream, my father was playing the piano, a Beethoven something, in a large concert hall which was filled with people. I was in the audience and I was reading a book. I suddenly realized that this was the wrong thing to do when my father was performing, so I sat up and paid attention. He was playing very well, I thought. Suddenly the conductor stopped the performance and began to sing a passage for my father, a passage that my father had evidently botched. My father listened attentively, smiling at the conductor.

Q: Does your father play? In actuality?

A: Not a note.

Q: Did the conductor resemble anyone you know?

A: No.

Q: What did you do, after work, in the evenings or on weekends, in Philadelphia?

A: Just ordinary things.

Q: No special interests?

A: I was very interested in bow-hunting. These new bows they have now, what they call a compound bow— Also, I'm a member of the Galapagos Society, we work for the environment, it's really a very effective—

Q: And what else?

A: Well, adultery. I would say that's how I spent most of my free time. In adultery.

Q: You mean regular adultery.

A: Yes. Sleeping with people although legally bound to someone else.

Q: These were women.

A: Invariably.

Q: And so that's what you did, in the evenings or on weekends. . . .

A: I had this strange experience. Today is Saturday, right? I called up this haircutter I go to, her name is Ruth, and asked her for an appointment. I needed a haircut. So she said she had openings at ten, ten-thirty, eleven, eleven-thirty, twelve, twelve-thirty—on a Saturday. Do you think the world knows something I don't know?

Q: It's possible.

A: What if she stabs me in the ear with the scissors?

Q: Unlikely, I would think.

A: Stabs me in the ear with the scissors in an excess of rage?

Q: Your guilt. I recognize it. Clearly, guilt.

A: Nonsense. The prudent man guards his eardrums. The prudent man avoids anomalous circumstances.

Q: You regard yourself as prudent.

A: I regard myself as asleep. I go along, things happen to me, there are disturbances, one copes, thinking of the golden pillow, I don't mean literally golden but golden in my esteem—

Q: Let me play this track here for you, it's by Echo and the Bunnymen—

A: I'll pass.

Q: I also have a video of the Tet offensive with Walter Cronkite . . .

"He's not potent more than forty-two percent of the time."

"Maybe we could feed him nourishing broths."

"They say that vitamin E is good for that."

"That's what I hear too."

"What if we give him too much vitamin E and it poisons him?"

"I don't think you can give somebody too much of any particular vitamin. The body takes what it needs and rejects the rest I read about it."

"It's because he's so old."

"I don't think so I read about this guy who was ninety-three and still was fathering children when he was ninety-three."

48

"Perhaps at long intervals after he had been carefully fed with vitamin E and nourishing broths."

"Maybe we should offer stimulating photographs."

"Of what?"

"Potentially arousing scenes."

"You mean the photographs would be more arousing than we are?"

"Well I don't know how their minds work."

"Maybe we should offer him potentially arousing scenes that are not photographs."

"You mean like real life."

"That's what I mean."

"Consisting of what?"

"I don't know I'd have to look in some books."

"He's doing the best he can."

"That's your opinion."

"I think he works quite hard at it, spends hours and hours."

"I just think we've gotten ourselves into a fundamentally false position here, I don't blame the poor bastard it's just more than the male mechanism is equipped to do."

"I saw this guy in a movie once I couldn't believe it."

"They have these special guys they use for those movies they're not what you usually run into. They're specialists."

"We don't want to stress him beyond his capacity or have him go mad or something."

"He shows no signs of going mad."

"He's raveling his clothes. Plucking at threads."

"I just think that means he doesn't have very good clothes. His clothes have a lot of loose ends and it's natural, I think, when you see a loose end to pluck at it."

"I use Lubriderm on him sometimes, that helps."

"I've noticed you've been buying a lot of Lubriderm."

"I share it what are you getting so het up about?"

"I haven't heard that expression since I was a child. Het up."

"Well we're mature women we should be able to cope with this."

"Has he made a will?"

"That's an evil thought, has he anything to will?"

"Beats me I wouldn't take it if he did."

"Sure you would."

"He could be more tan his red color is from drinking I'll bet a nickel."

"Not a perfect deal he's an animate wreck."

"Well I'll tell you I've never had that many orgasms with anybody else to give the devil his due."

"Well if you want simple frottage."

"He does appreciate what he's given."

"As well he should he's in hog heaven, objectively speaking."

"Where are we?"

"We're in some sort of waiting room. Waiting."

"How old is he actually?"

"He says he's fifty-three."

ONCE when he had come home with Carol early from a concert a police car was parked outside the house, so they hurried. Inside on the couch with the babysitter there was a half-naked policeman. He had retained his uniform trousers. His gunbelt was on the coffee table and the babysitter's blouse on the coffee table, a bottle of Dewar's there as well, "This is Rob," the babysitter said, and they said, "Hi, Rob." What breasts, Simon thought. He went into the kitchen and mixed himself a Gelusil and Carol went searching for a faraway closet to hang her black-beaded jacket in.

Rob removed himself into the felon-thick night, Carol gave the babysitter twelve dollars, and Simon looked in on the sleeping Sarah. She had kicked the

51

covers off and he replaced them. "Do you think he was on duty?" Carol asked, re-doing the covers.

"Yes," Simon said. "Did you say anything to her?"

"I didn't think it was necessary. She was blushing all over. Never seen a stomach blush like that."

"Did he leave the bottle?"

"No, took it."

"I think I'll call the chief. Fill him in on this matter."

"Oh, come on."

"What is she, fifteen?"

"Fully fifteen."

"A ripe fifteen."

"I saw." She led the way to the kitchen. "I guess that's Sarah eleven years from now."

"Oh misery me."

"You want to jump the babysitter."

"Where does this word 'jump' come from?"

"I know you."

"I don't think I've ever said that to anybody. 'I know you.' "

"You're too wrapped up in your own stuff even to try. To know someone."

"The phrase is a bit total. As in, 'I totaled the Buick.' "

"You worry about the way I say things but you don't worry about what I mean."

"That's not so. Anyhow, I don't want to screw the babysitter."

"You would if you could."

"Maybe in a state of nature. Philadelphia is not a state of nature."

"You're dumb. You're just *dumb*, Simon."

"I didn't hire the babysitter."

"She was highly recommended."

"Had this guy today tell me he was the fourth generation of his family to lose money in the cattle business. A client. What he was really saying was that he was cattle aristocracy and he made enough from his oil leases so that he could run two thousand head of cattle as a hobby. That's known as self-deprecating humor."

"You're changing the subject."

"It needs changing."

In bed, he was almost asleep. She came in and threw four quarts of icewater at him.

VERONICA is bouncing on her trampoline. Dore is reading *Flowers for Algernon*. Simon is in bed with Anne.

"You're about as tender as a sea lion," she says. "Have you ever done this before?"

"I remember having done it before."

"How does it make you feel with us in here and them out there?"

"Nervous."

"We're very tolerant."

"I see that. What's that wham-wham-wham noise?"

"Veronica."

"Is she making obscene comment?"

"She's just mindless when she gets on that trampo-

line. She can go for hours. She thinks she's got a problem with her rear. I don't think there's a problem but
she thinks there's a problem."

"Makes me nervous."

"Everything makes you nervous."

"True."

"Is this a male fantasy for you? This situation?"

"It's not a fantasy, is it."

"It has the structure of a male fantasy."

"The dumbest possible way to look at it."

"Well screw you."

"Our purpose here, I thought."

She turns him around and rubs his ass with her cunt
in long swooping motions.

"Where did you go to school?"

"Here and there."

"What did you learn?"

"Lots of important stuff. Almost everybody I've met
since was present in my first-grade class. Maybe thirty-
two kids in that class. Every type represented. When I
run into somebody who was not present in my first-
grade class I think I've sighted a rare bird."

"Where did you go to college? Was it Harvard?"

"No it wasn't Harvard."

"Lots of people didn't go to Harvard."

"There's just not enough Harvard."

"Maybe they could start a branch. In Florida or
somewhere."

"They probably don't feel the urgency."

"What's redeye gravy?"

"Ham drippings with a splash of coffee."

"Can we make some?"

"Go ahead."

"Blackeyed peas?"

"I love blackeyed peas."

"Collard greens."

"Fine."

"We'll need some corn likker."

"Try the likker store."

"Be good if we had some hounds lazing about."

"I draw the line at hounds."

"Simon, I'm trying to do this thing right."

"I know you are."

She looks beautiful, her long dark hair done up in a ponytail. Her ARM THE UNEMPLOYED t-shirt.

"What are you going to do after we leave?" she asks.

"Go back to work, I guess."

"That what you want to do?"

"Work is God's best invention. Keeps you all seized up and interested."

"I wish I could do something."

"You could always go to school."

"I don't like standing in lines."

"I know what you mean. The Army used up most of my standing-in-line capacity."

"But suppose you're at a reception and you're going to meet the President and there's a long line of very well-dressed people—"

"I'm not in a hurry to meet the President. If he wants to come over and have a drink and a little guacamole dip, that's fine. My door is always open."

"You don't care about anything."

"Listening to the radio."

"You do love your radios."

"I'm thinking of getting another one. They have these waterproof jobs for the bath—"

"I like a quiet reflective bath."

"I'll come in and put toads in the water."

"Where would you get toads in New York City?"

"Toad store. They got big toads, little toads, horned toads, no-horn toads—"

"It's a great city."

"It's a great argument for cities."

SIMON wanted very much to be a hearty, optimistic American, like the President, but on the other hand did not trust hearty, optimistic Americans, like the President. He had considered the possibility that the President, when not in public, was not really hearty and optimistic but rather a gloomy, obsessed man with a profound fear of the potentially disastrous processes in which he was enmeshed, no more sanguine than the Fisher King. He did not really believe this to be the case. He himself had settled for being a competent, sometimes inventive architect with a tragic sense of brick. Brick was his favorite material as the fortress was the architectural metaphor that he had, more and more, to resist. To force himself into freshness, he thought about bamboo.

Getting old, Simon. Not so limber, dear friend, time for the bone factory? The little blue van. Your hands are covered with tiny pepperoni. Your knees predict your face. Your back stabs you, on the left side, twice a day. The belly's been discussed. The soul's shrinking to a microdot. We're ordering your rocking chair, size 42. Would you like something in Southern pine? Loblolly? Send the women away. They're too good for you. Also, not good for you. Are you King Solomon? Your kingdom a scant two hundred fifty-nine thousand, two hundred square inches. Annual tearfall, three and one-quarter inches. You feedeth among the lilies, Simon. There are garter snakes among the lilies, Simon, garter belts too. Your garden is over-cultivated, it needs weeds. How's your skiwear, Simon? Done any demolition derbies lately? You run the mile in, what, a year and a half? We're sending you an electric treadmill, a solid steel barbell curl bar, a digital pedometer. Use them. And send the women away.

When he asked himself what he was doing, living in a bare elegant almost unfurnished New York apartment with three young and beautiful women, Simon had to admit that he *did not know* what he was doing. He was, he supposed, listening. These women were taciturn as cowboys, spoke only to the immediate question, probably did not know in which century the Second World War had taken place. No, too hard; it was, rather, that what they knew was so wildly various, ragout of Spinoza and Cyndi Lauper with a William Buckley sherbet floating in the middle of it. He'd come in one evening to find all three of them kneeling on the dining room table with their rumps pointing at him. Obviously he was supposed to strip off his gentlemanly khakis and attend to all three at once, just as obviously an impossibility. He had placed a friendly hand on each cul in turn and said, "Okay, guys, you've had your fun, now get back to the barracks and polish the Renoirs." *That boy has no talent,* muttered Manet to Monet one afternoon in the garden, about Renoir. "Out, out, out," he'd shouted, and they'd scattered, giggling. One night on his back in bed he'd had six breasts to suck, swaying above him, he was poor tattered Romulus. When they couldn't get a part of him they'd play with each other.

SIMON and Dore sitting in the kitchen. The radio making music.

"They play the best music late at night," Dore said. "When they think nobody's awake."

"That's Keith Jarrett."

"Who's he?"

"Piano player. Very famous."

"What's that funny noise?"

"He kinds of sings when he plays."

"Oh. I guess you old guys know a lot of different stuff, don't you. How old are you?"

"Fifty-three."

"You don't look it. You look maybe fifty, fifty-one. That was good chicken we had."

"Thank you."

"I wrung a neck once. In Fort Lupton. It was a mess."

"By hand?"

"All the way off. It was a mess."

"Now they use electrocution."

"I read about it."

"All the chickens hooked into this moving contrivance—"

"Their heads dangling in water—"

"Then whfft! whfft! whfft!"

"It's horrible."

"The father chicken says to the son chicken, Son, I've got bad news for you."

"Then, whfft!"

"This country runs on chicken."

"Just think of it. A little bird like that. Fueling the nation."

"At night, in the great chicken factories, whfft! whfft! whfft! whfft! All through the night."

"They don't do it in the daytime?"

"Under cover of night. So people don't realize the extent."

"If I was a chicken I'd fly away. Before they got me."

"They're bum fliers. A ham can fly better."

"How do they kill the hams?"

"You don't want to know."

"Simon. You're not a serious man."

"Yes I am."

Dore likes to scold people. When anyone in the

house does anything that does not meet her specifications for appropriate behavior, Dore scolds.

"Simon you're not supposed to talk to Anne like that."

"Like what?"

"You were condescending."

"In what way?"

"Okay, she never heard of the Marshall Plan. You don't have to explain it to her. In that way."

"Was I pompous?"

"Not more than usual. It was that incredulous look. Like you couldn't believe that somebody'd never heard of the Marshall Plan."

"It was a big deal, historically."

"Simon you are twice as old as we are."

"That does not absolve you of the necessity of knowing your own history."

"That's pompous. That's truly pompous. That's just what I'm talking about. And another thing."

"Oh Lord, what?"

"When you made that joke about George Gershwin and his lovely wife, Ira."

"Well?"

"Anne didn't know it was a joke. You can't make jokes that are based on people not knowing things. It's not fair. It's demeaning to women."

"Why to women?"

"Women don't pay that much attention to silly things like that. All that detail. And there's one more thing."

"Which is?"

"You should take the laundry sometimes. Just because we're women doesn't mean that we have to take the laundry all the time."

"Okay. Good point."

"We don't like sitting in that tacky laundromat any better than you do."

"I told you to leave it and let them do it."

"You save for four people's clothes eight to ten dollars. I think that's significant."

"But you don't have to do it that way."

"Also I met this interesting guy there last time. He's a professional whistler."

H<small>E'S</small> listening to one of his three radios, this one a brutish black Proton with an outboard second speaker. The announcer is talking about drummers. "Cozy Cole comes straight out of Chick Webb," he says. Simon nods in agreement. "Big Sid Catlett. Zutty Singleton, Dave Tough. To go even further back, Baby Dodds. All this before we get to Krupa and Buddy Rich." Simon taxes his memory in an attempt to extract from it the names of, ten additional drummers. Louis Bellson. Shelly Manne. Panama Francis. Jo Jones, of course. Kenny Clarke. Elvin Jones. Barrett Deems. Mel Lewis. Charlie Persip. Joe Morello. Next, twenty bass players. Our nation is rich in talent, he thinks.

He calls his mother in California.

"What do we do with brisket?" he asks.

"What fool bought brisket?"

"A friend."

His mother understands what this means. "You've got to boil the hell out of it," she says. "How many pounds?"

"Four."

"I'd give it three and a half to four hours in stock with carrots. Never did see the point of carrots but they must be good for something. Slice an onion and put in some red wine. What's your friend's name?"

"They're just some people who're staying here temporarily."

"How's Sarah?"

"Doing well. She got a General Electric fellowship. Four thousand bucks."

"Every little bit helps," his mother says. "You and Carol speaking to each other?"

"At intervals. She's very busy."

"Does she have a friend?"

"Probably. I don't know."

"Make a sauce for it with capers, horseradish, mayonnaise and some of the cooking stock. Chill the sauce, it's best cold. That's all I know about brisket. You could stick some red cabbage into the pot for the last thirty minutes of cooking. Also, if I were you I'd buy some Union Carbide."

"Why?"

"Do what your mother tells you," she says, and hangs up.

PARADISE

His mother likes to present herself as a tough old bird, and in fact, that's the way he thinks of her. But there is a lustrous photograph of his mother sitting by the side of a pool in the 30s, radiating a formidable sexuality. Then no tough old bird but rather a bad, bad article, ready for Clark Gable and Lord Mountbatten, too.

N<small>EW</small> architecture is "soulless," Simon reads, again and again and again. He has trouble disagreeing when what is being talked about is a seventy-story curtain-wall building on Sixth Avenue. People don't like to live or work above the second floor in any building, the third at the outer extreme. No building should be taller than a ship. People like light; on the other hand, they also like caves. An austere façade pleases architects; people like decoration, a modicum of drama. Embassies are now being designed like banks, with more and more security as one moves deeper and deeper into the building, the most secure space, deep inside, mighty like a vault. Reconcile that with the idea of an embassy as a pleasing, friendly presence. Metal detectors set up at the entrances of schools. Gun-toting Wackenhuts in supermarkets (part of the design). Enter a jewelry store and above the selling floor there's a booth with bulletproof glass with gun ports and a guy with a shotgun. Giant concrete flowerpots all around the Capitol which have nothing to do with love of flowers. The messianic-maniacal idea that architecture will make people better, civilize them, central to much 1920s–1930s architectural thought, Corbusier, Gropius, even Wright, abandoned. Although modesty is not what architects do best, there is more restraint now, Simon thinks. I'll do my piece of the problem and you do yours. Not at all soulless, rather more cottage industry, S.O.M. notwithstanding. The image that seems to him really on the mark is the circus.

"Man's chief end is to glorify God and to enjoy Him forever," says his radio. He's been listening to a lot of Christian rock lately, finds it surprisingly robust. *Jesus is rock in a weary land.* He wonders how, say, Dodo Marmarosa would sound playing Christian rock. Dore comes in and shoves a breast in his ear. He makes a sound like a smoke alarm.

He has something cut off his forehead, a skin cancer that's been there for years, a dark spot the diameter of a pencil eraser. The doctor is a tall gloomy man with a Southern accent. He doesn't waste time, has Simon on the table and is scraping away with a curette within two minutes. First, four sharp stings as he places the lidocaine; afterward, the smell of burning brain as he cauterizes the blood vessels.

Simon writes a check for eighty-five dollars. He walks back to the apartment from the doctor's office, something like sixty-five blocks. It's cool and cloudy out. Bumptious loudmouthed swaggering teenagers coming down the street, jostling people. Simon sidesteps them. *Can't shoot 'em all.* An absolutely beautiful woman in blue walking toward him. He turns and looks after her. She walks on without turning. Well, why should she? He's fifty-three.

WHEN Simon wonders what kind of animal he is, he identifies with the giraffe. An improbable design, a weird ensemble overall, no special reputation for wisdom, an uncle-figure at best. Neglected by the auto industry: no Ford Giraffes on the highways. Simon too has a long neck, often commented upon, and a peculiar gait, sort of a shamble.

He gets a call from his wife, Carol, in Philadelphia.

"You haven't paid the car insurance," she says. "On either car. I got stopped by a cop yesterday and he jacked me up about the insurance."

"What'd you get stopped for?"

"Taillight."

"Call Bud at the office and tell him to take care of

71

it," Simon says. "He's got all the paperwork on the insurance. How are you?"

"Considering what our mayor is up to, I'm reasonably sane. This thing is really working out much better than I thought it would. Your being gone, I mean."

"The absence of a plan is itself a plan," Simon says. "Heard from Sarah?"

"She called a day or so ago. She's dropped German and history."

"Oh Lord. Why history?"

"They had to write papers."

"She can hardly avoid writing papers."

"She needs a typewriter."

"Buy her a typewriter."

"Simon, I've got other things to do. I'll give her a check but I can't futz around shopping for typewriters."

"Okay, fine. Is she happy?"

"She's been going out with some kind of Finn. I think he's a Finn. Very goodlooking. He's in the business school."

"How's his English?"

"Very Brit. What are you doing?"

"Reading. Walking around."

"Chasing tail."

"No I'm not chasing anything."

"It was just a sociological observation. I don't care."

"I know that."

"Keep in touch."

"I will."

"Your bad brother," Simon says to Dore. "Why is he in New York?"

"Nothing for him in Denver, he thinks. He's thirty-three. Two years in jail for auto theft. He's on probation now. He deals when he can get enough money to buy something to deal. He's good at calculating how often he can hit people up. He has me down for a couple of hundred every three months or so. His name is Burt."

She holds out an empty wineglass. Simon pouring.

"He's an engineer, actually. He designed this electric car, where you didn't have an array of batteries that had to be charged every two or three days. It had a circuit that allowed the batteries to recharge themselves just like gas engines recharge their batteries. There was a tiny computer in there somewhere. That was the car he stole. He was in partnership with these guys who'd put up the development money and when the prototype worked, they cut him out of the company. So he repossessed the car one night but they had the cops waiting for him."

"Couldn't he have started up again after he got out?"

"He forgot how he did it. He'd hurt his brain, drinking busthead in jail. He tried, drove himself crazy trying. He's still trying."

"Bad luck."

"Yeah. It could do ninety on the highway, too. My family is not exactly a blue-chip outfit."

She takes his glass out of his hand. "You drink too much."

"Goddamnit woman, leave my glass alone."

"I'd hate to see your liver."

"Most unlikely that you ever will."

"And I don't like it that when we have roast lamb you take all the crackling for yourself."

"Anything else?"

"Yes. This place isn't clean."

"So clean it."

"It's a matter of setting an example. You're the *jefe grande* around here."

"What's that mean?"

"Big chief."

"Not what I feel like."

"I'm talking basic reality."

A: I sometimes think of myself as a person who, you know what I mean, could have done something else, it doesn't matter what particularly. Just something else. I saw an ad in the Sunday paper for the CIA, a recruiting ad, maybe a quarter of a page, and I suddenly thought, it might be interesting to do that. Even though I've always been opposed to the CIA, when they were trying to bring Cuba down, the stuff with Lumumba in Africa, the stuff in Central America ... Then here is this ad, perfectly straightforward, "where your career is America's strength" or something like that, "aptitude for learning a foreign language is a plus" or something like that, I've always been good at languages, and I'm sitting there thinking about how my

75

résumé might look to them, starting completely over in something completely new, changing the very sort of person I am, and there was an attraction, a definite attraction. Of course the maximum age was thirty-five. I guess they want them more malleable.

Q: So, in the evenings or on weekends—

A: Not every night or every weekend. I mean this depended on the circumstances. Sometimes my wife and I went to dinner with people, or watched television—

Q: But in the main—

A: It wasn't that often. It was once in a while.

Q: Adultery is a sin.

A: It is classified as a sin, yes. Absolutely.

Q: The Sixth Commandment says—

A: I know what it says. I was raised on the Sixth Commandment. But.

Q: But what?

A: The Sixth Commandment is wrong.

Q: It's wrong?

A: It's wrong.

Q: The whole Commandment?

A: I don't know how it happened, whether it's a mistranslation from the Aramaic or whatever, it may not even have been Aramaic I don't know, I certainly do not pretend to scholarship in this area but my sense of the matter is that the Sixth Commandment is an error.

Q: Well if that were true it would change quite a lot of things, wouldn't it?

A: Take the pressure off, a bit.

Q: Have you told your wife?

A: Yes, Carol knows.

Q: How'd she take it?

A: Well, she *liked* the Sixth Commandment. You could reason that it was in her interest to support the Sixth Commandment for the preservation of the family unit and this sort of thing but to reason that way is, I would say, to take an extremely narrow view of Carol, of what she thinks. She's not predictable. She once told me that she didn't want me, she wanted a suite of husbands, ten or twenty—

Q: What did you say?

A: I said, Go to it.

Q: Myself, I think about being just sort of a regular person, one who worries about cancer a lot, every little thing a prediction of cancer, no I don't want to go for my every-two-years-checkup because what if they find something? I wonder what will kill me and when it will happen and how it will happen, and I wonder about my parents, who are still alive, and what will happen to them. This seems to me to be a proper set of things to worry about. Last things.

A: I don't think God gives a snap about adultery. This is just an opinion, of course.

Q: So how do you, how shall I put it, pursue—

A: You think about this staggering concept, the mind of God, and then you think He's sitting around worrying about this guy and this woman at the Beechnut Travelodge? I think not.

Q: Well He doesn't have to think about every particular instance, He just sort of laid out the general principles—

A: He also created creatures who, with a single powerful glance—

Q: The eyes burn.

A: They do.

Q: The heart leaps.

A: Like a terrapin.

Q: Stupid youth returns.

A: Like hockey sticks falling out of a long-shut closet.

Q: Do you play?

A: I did. Many years ago.

Q: You find them in parks. You blunder upon them in parks.

A: I've noticed that.

Q: They sit in parks a lot. Especially when they're angry. The solitary bench. Shoulders raised, legs kicking—

WHEN he was in school at Penn, the resident master was Louis Kahn. Kahn was given to muttering. Once he stood behind Simon's draughting table and muttered for almost five minutes. The young architect was too intimidated to ask him what he was saying. The story was told of Kahn that when *he* was a young architect he had worked for Paul Cret, the French maestro who presided at Penn in the 20s. When the other draughtsmen, thirty of them, quit for the day Kahn would take a roll of tracing paper and go from board to board, leaving critiques of each architect's work as an overlay. He did not neglect the boards of the firm's three principals.

I love the excesses of my profession, Simon thought,

heroics and mock-heroics. Michael Graves and Robert Venturi, *Complexity and Contradiction* as a text. All those form-givers enjoying themselves as Michelangelo, Wright and his cape, Mies and his pinstripes. Michelangelo most of all: "Where I steal I leave a knife." An appropriate High Renaissance sentiment. The walls of the architecture labs at Penn had been covered with graffiti. "This is hell, nor are we out of it." "Hell is other architects." "The road to hell is paved with naugahyde."

White underwear with golden skin. Acres and acres of it. Was it golden? Conventionally described as golden. The color of white birch stained with polyurethane. What do we think of this color combination? Some people vote for black underwear with such skin but these people are the same people who paint their bathrooms black. Walking in the garden, Modigliani said to Saint-Gaudens, about Renoir, "This roughneck will never be a painter." Dressed women, half-dressed women, quarter-dressed women. Simon was, as the women repeatedly told him, existing in a male fantasy, in hog heaven. He saw nothing wrong with male fantasies (the Taj Mahal, the Chrysler Building) but denied that he was in hog heaven. Where did they get such expressions? A Southernism that he'd not heard in thirty years.

IN the mornings, large figures shrouded in terrycloth lurch back and forth between the several bedrooms and the single bathroom. Dore runs, in the mornings, picks up breakfast at the market on the way back, fresh Italian rolls, green garlicked Kräuterbutter, a quarter-pound of breast of veal. She has become the manager of breakfast, takes pride in varying the fare, fine cheeses one day, a decadent kidney stew the next, blueberry crepes and then chicken-fried steak with beaten biscuits. "This breaded burlap," Veronica says, "nicely done, but what are you, trying to kill us, or what?"

"Try more pepper."

Still in her sweats, she washes the dishes and stows

them away, then settles down with the Business Day section of the *Times,* Revco Gets $1.16 Billion Buyout Bid, Troubled Farm Banks to Get Regulatory Aid, Japanese Setback on Chip Prices. Scratching a bare foot with one hand, flipping pages with the other. Then she showers, dips into MTV (shoulder to shoulder with Anne for fifteen minutes). Then's she off to the New School for her Tuesday class, *Investment Strategies for the Eighties.*

"How'd you get in?" Simon asks.

"I'm auditing," she says. "I go early and get a seat. The class is so big they never take the roll."

"You getting anything out of it?"

"You can't play unless you have something to play with. Still, it's educational."

After class, her nap. She throws herself on her bed and is dead to the world for an hour and a half, wearing only spun-sugar V-shaped briefs by Olga. Simon stares, on occasion, at the beautiful body at rest, face down on the bed. What miracles of bawdiness it can perform without thinking, the operator quite unaware. In sleep, she scratches her belly. He feels the urge to sit on the edge of the bed (hurl himself into the bed), but does not. At night, she either puts herself together for Fizz or reads Dickens. She's bought four Dickens novels in worn Everyman editions at the Strand and is moving through them methodically. "The thing about Dickens is," she tells him, "he knew the value of a pound, when you didn't have one. All his people are scrambling for money."

"So?" Simon says.

"I identify with that."

Late at night she sits with Simon drinking a Dos Equis and listening to Horace Silver.

"You're the mother of these guys," he says.

"I'm not. Last among equals."

"Veronica's a handful."

"She's her own person. I admire her. She's the smartest."

"How long have you three known each other?"

Dore giggles. "We all worked for a retail outlet in Denver. It was called Frederick's of Hollywood of Denver. It had nothing to do with the real Frederick's of Hollywood."

"Is that clothes?"

"Yes. Clothes."

Dore knows one trick which may one day place her among the world's managers, how to walk. Dore always walks briskly, head up, arms swinging in good military style, moving from one very important assignment to the next, a bit rushed, look-what-those-apes-in-Purchasing-have-done-to-us-now. Simon, having spent some time in large organizations, understands what Dore's walk means, can appreciate its brittle bouncy R.A.F. authority. Veronica dawdles and Anne lurches, although at moments of confusion all lurch, banging into each other as if blindfolded. Simon shambles.

Veronica is often out on mysterious errands which the others do not comment upon. What is she doing? Simon tries not to think about this—it's none of his business—but he can't help speculating. Is she taking a shift as a blackjack dealer in Atlantic City? Loading container ships in Hoboken? Re-fletching arrows at the Museum of the American Indian? Pushing commodities in a bucket shop on Varick Street? The darker possibilities he refuses to contemplate. She enters in a flurry, having missed dinner, and declares she's starving. Simon plops a stuffed pork chop on her plate, wild rice, white asparagus. Dore and Anne scarcely notice her, they're talking about life after death.

"No way," Anne says, "do I want to live after death. It's hard enough as it is."

"But you're not close to the end yet," says Dore. "The end is not near. When the end is near, you may feel differently."

"I doubt it. An eternity of keeping the armpits tidy? No thank you."

"The grave's a fine and quiet place. That's not it. The grave's a fine and pleasant place. That's not it. What is it, Simon?"

"Don't know."

"Private," says Veronica. "The grave's a fine and private place. I remember that one. He goes on to say that there's no sex in the grave."

"But what if you leap over the grave and into something new? Something that has been imagined only by saints and mendicant friars in their robes of grass and rope?"

"Like what?" Anne says. "Some kind of church thing? I never did like church."

"Church is punishment for our sins," Dore says,

84

"everybody knows that. The only question is whether by the time you die you've done enough church to be punished enough."

"I haven't," Veronica says. "I dropped out when I was ten. Actually they asked my mother to leave because she was living in sin with my father and had been for ten years and they decided it was too flagrant."

"What denomination was that?" Anne asks.

"Assembly of God. Their motto was 'The Fellowship of Excitement.' It was very exciting when they threw my mother out. A committee called on her and told her. There were three men and two women. She served apple juice and chocolate-chip cookies. All she said afterward was that it was a waste of apple juice."

"I kind of liked it," Dore said. "I guess it was my authoritarian personality. We were Lutheran. A rare bunch, the Lutherans, they take everything very seriously. What were you, Simon?"

"A simple Presbyterian."

Veronica places five hundred-dollar bills on the table. "A little contribution to the household economy."

"Where in the world did you get that?"

"It wasn't hooking."

"So, where?"

"O.T.B."

"You bastard! What was the horse?"

"Crushed Rose."

SIMON buys an artwork. The artwork is a print by the artist John Chamberlain and depicts a lot of automobile bumpers smashed together into a sculptural block. It's very small, ten inches square, modestly framed. He has trouble placing it on the big empty walls of the apartment; wherever he puts it, it looks ridiculous. Finally he hangs it by the front door.

Anne looks at it. "What's that?"

"A print."

"Who by?"

"Guy named Chamberlain."

"Not very big."

"No it's not."

She moves closer for a good look. "Car bumpers."

86

"Yes."

"I like it."

"So do I."

"Terribly small. For this big wall."

"This is not the Frick."

"Looks funny all alone like that."

"A brave little picture. Holds the wall."

"I guess if you like it and I like it, that's all that counts."

She turns and holds out her hand.

"Sweet of you to try."

"We can get more. One of these days."

"Maybe just have this one. Symbolizing the situation."

"What do you mean by the situation?"

"We have hot dogs for dinner."

"How did you know I wanted hot dogs?"

"I just intuited it."

"Getting pretty domestic around here."

She's flipping a kitchen knife around and catching it by the blade in a dangerous manner.

"I guess. Still, we know the truth."

Sarah calls.

"Who was that who answered the phone?" she asks.

"That was Anne."

"Who's she?"

"A guest. I was in the kitchen."

"Bluebeard."

"How are you?"

"I got a new typewriter."

"What kind?"

"Smith-Corona. It can spell fifty thousand words right."

"More than I can spell right."

"Me too. I got pregnant. Mom tell you?"

"No. She didn't."

"Then I spontaneously aborted. Last month."

"She should have told me. Or you should have told me."

"No big deal."

"This the guy from Finland?"

"Yeah. He went back."

"His reindeer were on fire."

"He was going back anyhow. I told him to go."

"How do you feel?"

"I'm not having world-class luck."

"Probably there's something wrong with you," Simon says. "Some kind of character flaw, final and ineradicable."

"That's it," she says. "You coming home any time soon?"

"It'll be a while yet," he says. "Sweetie, you can come over here. Whenever you want."

"Scared of what I might see," she says. "So long."

SIMON remembered Sarah screaming when he tried to turn off the television set. The thing had captured her and anyone who laid a hand on it was subject to a full-scale tantrum with kettle drums and cannon. She was, for some reason, inordinately fond of Daffy Duck, although the Road Runner was also a favorite. She was queenly in expressing herself. At two, she produced a sentence that Simon still marveled at. When events were not marching to her satisfaction she would say, gravely, *"You are making me angry."* After this sentence joined the household's sentence-hoard Simon ceased to worry about language acquisition. In the early mornings she would rush into the bedroom and climb into bed with Simon and his wife, settling in between them with soft little groans of satisfaction. When she grew up, she said, she wanted to be a ballerina. Her mother made her a tutu out of some pink gauzy material and she pranced about the house in this, white Danskins, and a cardboard tiara on which gold stars had been pasted, exhibiting all the grace of a tall gesturing cactus. When she was fourteen she was picked up for shoplifting, frightened as thoroughly as possible, and released. The item in question was a tube of lip gloss called Penumbra.

He remembered Carol jumping on him for using the mitt to hold the end of the veal bone while he tried to cut meat from it. *"That's not what the mitt is for!"* He had told her to shut up, it was his mitt, he'd use it for any damned thing he cared to including cleaning the grease trap if he cared to. Mitt nights. After dinner she told him not to eat onions from the pot. The baby standing on the kitchen table and singing

> I'm pretty
> I'm pretty
> And I don't care

Memories of mitt.

"This guy slapped Veronica."

"Why?"

"She doesn't know. She went out for pizza and stopped at the Korean market. She had a big cauliflower in her hands, she was kind of feeling it to see if it was—"

"And he slapped her?"

"A black guy. Walked up to her and slapped her in the face. Knocked her sunglasses off."

"What'd she do?"

"He was a Vietnam vet."

"How do you know?"

"He said so. He said, 'I'm a Vietnam vet and I'm crazy.' Then he slapped her. Then he asked her for money."

"Did she give him any?"

"Of course not, she threw the cauliflower at him."

"Did it hit him?"

"No it hit an old lady. Right in the mush. She didn't throw it so well?"

"What happened then?"

"The Korean guy behind the counter had a fit. Fell down and foamed at the mouth."

"Is he okay?"

"The paramedics took him away."

"What happened to the black guy?"

"He split."

"Is Veronica okay?"

"Sure. She's used to it. Being bashed around. This is a great town you have here."

Dore is angry. She's holding the box that the frozen pizza came in.

"You're actually going to feed us this pizza?"

"What's the matter with it?"

"This frozen pizza?"

"So it's frozen."

"Do you know what it's got in it? Enriched flour."

"What's the matter with enriched flour?"

"The enriched flour has in it flour, niacin, reduced iron, thiamine mononitrate, and riboflavin."

"All great stuff. I remember riboflavin from my childhood. They put it in Wheaties or something."

"We're just getting started. We're just going into our windup here. We get water, hydrogenated soybean oil, yeast, salt, and something called dough conditioner. The dough conditioner's got sodium stearoyl lactylate, calcium sulfate and sodium sulfite."

"Soybeans are good. Invented by Martin Luther King."

"Moving right along, we get cooked pork and mozzarella cheese substitute. The mozzarella cheese substitute contains water, casein, hydrogenated soybean oil—you notice the soybean is doing a lot of work here—salt, sodium aluminum phosphate, lactic acid, natural flavor whatever that is, modified cornstarch, sodium citrate, sorbic acid, sodium phosphate, artificial color, guar gum, magnesium oxide, ferric orthophosphate, zinc oxide, B-12, folic acid, B-6 hydrochloride, niacinamide, vitamin A palmitate, xanthan gum, thiamine mononitrate—I ask you."

"What?"

"Is this food or a chemistry set?"

"Doesn't taste too bad."

"I could make a nuclear weapon with less stuff than this pizza has in it."

A bare leg against a purplish sheet.

The thing is, they *discuss* him.

"He could lose maybe fifteen pounds."

"I think it's kind of cute. Like Santa Claus with what does it say a bowl full of jelly."

"Good shoulders. Deep chest. That's in his favor."

"And he's got good posture. Were you ever in the service, Simon?"

"Two years."

"When was that?"

"In the 50s."

"You do anything?"

"Of a military nature? No, I just put in my time."

"A little bowlegged don't you think?"

"It's not bowlegs it's just that the knees are too close together."

"Big feet."

"Well he's a big boy."

"The hands look a little toilworn to my eye."

"You need to use some kind of lotion, Simon, Lubriderm or—"

"But he's still got pretty much hair for a guy his age, that's a plus."

"I think you need a haircut, Simon, get away from that shaggy look, that's not the look of today."

"Veronica can cut it for you. Veronica knows how to cut hair."

"A five-buck tip, Simon, that's all it takes. Thirty for the haircut and five for the tip."

They say, over and over:

"Catch my drift?"

"Catch my drift?"

"Catch my drift?"

Anne says, "You never had to stand around in your frillies with all those guys looking at you."

"Well, that's true."

"Also, my boobs are too small."

"By what standard?"

"Generally accepted standards."

Her breasts are in fact quite perfect. "Look, dear friend," he says, "one would have to journey many days, cross mighty rivers and slog up and down towering mountains, cut through thick mato grossos with machetes in each hand, to find a more beautiful woman than your sweet self."

"Do you really think that?"

"Of course."

"Doesn't do me any good if I'm dumb, does it?"

"What makes you think you're dumb?"

"If I wasn't dumb I wouldn't be a professional model."

"Doesn't follow. Look at—" He gropes for the name of a model who is also amazingly intelligent but his knowledge of the field is inadequate. "Lauren Hutton," he says.

"She makes movies too."

"Tons of intelligence there," he says. "A glance convinces. Probably dreams three-dimensional chess. Q.E.D."

"You're very supportive, Simon."

"I love you guys."

"That's the first time you've said that."

"I slipped."

"We're in March now. This is March, right?"

"The sixteenth."

"We've been here what, a month?"

"Just about."

"So. Are you satisfied?"

"In what regard?"

"With us. Being here."

"Of course. Very much so."

"You're not going to boot us out."

"Why would I do that?"

"Maybe you don't like the deal."

"Do I seem itchy?"

"I can't tell with you. You've got a hard shell."

"Look, I'm fine. I don't think Veronica is too happy."

"Yeah, it's a problem. She's always been that way. She kind of expects the worst, you know? She's got an affinity for the worst. She seeks it out."

"Why?"

"It's her mind-set, I guess. She got knocked around a lot as a kid. She talks about it sometimes."

"People get over it."

"No they don't."

A: A dead bear in a blue dress, face down on the kitchen floor. I trip over it, in the dark, when I get up at 2 A.M. to see if there's anything to eat in the refrigerator. It's an architectural problem, marriage. If we could live in separate houses, and visit each other when we felt particularly gay— It would be expensive, yes. But as it was she had to endure me in all my worst manifestations, early in the morning and late at night and in the nutsy obsessed noontimes. When I wake up from my nap you don't *get* the laughing cavalier, you get a rank pigfooted belching blunderer. I knew this one guy who built a wall down the middle of his apartment. An impenetrable wall. He had a very big apartment. It worked out very well. Concrete block, basically, with fiberglass insulation on top of that and sheetrock on top of that.

Q: Well, how does it make you feel? Adultery.

A: There's a certain amount of guilt attached. I feel guilty. But I feel guilty even without adultery. I exist in a morass of guilt. There's maybe a little additional wallop of guilt but I already feel so guilty that I hardly notice it.

Q: Where does all this guilt come from? The extra-adulterous guilt?

A: I keep wondering if, say, there is intelligent life on other planets, the scientists argue that something like two percent of the other planets have the conditions, the physical conditions, to support life in the way it happened here, did Christ visit each and every planet, go through the same routine, the Agony in the Garden, the Crucifixion, and so on. . . . And these guys on these other planets, these life-forms, maybe they look like boll weevils or something, on a much larger scale of course, were they told that they shouldn't go to bed with other attractive six-foot boll weevils arrayed in silver and gold and with little squirts of Opium behind the ears? Doesn't make sense. But of course our human understanding is imperfect.

Q: You haven't answered me. This general guilt—

A: Yes, that's the interesting thing. I hazard that it is not guilt so much as it is inadequacy. I feel that everything is being nibbled away, because I can't *get it right*—

Q: Would you like to be able to fly?

A: It's crossed my mind.

Q: The women were a little strident don't you think?

A: No I don't think that.

Q: Sometimes a little strident?

A: Everybody's a little strident sometimes.

Q: Sometimes you have to scream to be heard. Isn't that what you think?

A: I don't think that.

Q: I never scream. I'm a doctor.

A: Your good fortune.

Q: It has nothing to do with good fortune. It has to do with years of the most strenuous intellectual effort. Were they strident in bed?

A: Different styles in bed as elsewhere. I guess you could call Veronica strident. Stridency is a response to dissatisfaction.

Q: Where is satisfaction?

A: In sleep?

WHAT if they all lived happily ever after together? An unlikely prospect. What was there in his brain that forbade such felicity? *Too much*, his brain said, but the brain was a fair-to-middling brain at best, the glucose that kept it marching, metabolized crème brûlée, was present but there was not enough vinegar in this brain, it lacked vinegar. Simon drank vinegar in the mornings from bottles sold to him as white wine and thought of Paris, where every fifteen-franc bottle was good, better than anything else he'd ever tasted. In Switzerland, in the summer, in Zurich and Basel, he'd found chilled red wine not bad either, a learning experience, also that he did not want to live in a country so ferociously tidy. The prostitutes in Zurich were hand-

some well-dressed zebras, favoring stark black and
white, street furniture ornamental as the staid perfect
cops or the show windows of the Bahnhofstrasse, much
gold winking behind heavy glass. He did not want a
watch or cufflinks or a gold-plated coffee service, he was
at a disadvantage. What was there to do with these
women? He'd send them all to MIT, make architects of
them! Women were coming into the profession in in-
creasing numbers. The group could chat happily about
mullions, in the evening by the fireside, tiring of mullions, turn to cladding, wearying of cladding, attack
with relish the problems of blast-cleaned pressure-
washed gun-applied polymer-cement-coated steel. Quel
happiness!

Someone would get pregnant, everyone would get
pregnant. At seventy he'd be dealing with Pampers and
new teeth. The new children would be named Susan-
nah, Clarice, and Buck. He'd stroll out on the lawn, in
the twilight, and throw the football at Buck. The football would rocket about two feet, then head for the
greensward. The pitiful little child would say "Kain't
anybody here play this game?"

LIGHTNING. Four o'clock in the afternoon. The women are in the kitchen, enjoying the display in the big windows.

Anne says, "What are we going to do about this bozo?"

"What's to do?" Veronica asks.

"He hasn't hurt anything. Yet," says Dore.

"He's been very circumspect."

"I think too circumspect."

"I think he thinks he's doing the right thing."

"I don't think he's a nut."

"I don't think he's a nut either."

"He likes those Windham Hill records."

"I don't think that makes him a nut."

102

"He uses too much butter when he cooks. He's making pasta, he throws half a stick of butter in just before he serves it."

"Butter makes everything taste better."

"He looks around to see if anyone's watching before he throws it in. Then he whips it around in there real quick. Hoping it will melt before anybody sees it."

"It's just an effort to raise the level. That kind of shows I think an effort to raise the level of life that's not too terrible. Typically American."

A majestic crash. They jump.

"That was a biggie."

"Not too bad."

"But what of us? What are we going to do?"

"Bide our time."

"I like that expression."

"Have you ever hung out with an architect before?"

"I knew this guy he was a contractor he contracted Port-O-Sans."

"What are they?"

"Movable outhouses."

"Good Lord this man is old."

"Fifty-three. Old enough to be our father."

"Yet he has a certain spirit."

"We've got to get something going."

"Like what?"

"Something."

"This town is creepy."

"It's so big and vast."

"What about the rabid skunks?"

"They found another one."

"Where?"

"At the Cloisters."

"Is that far away?"

"Way uptown. Fort Tryon Park."

"What was it doing?"

"It was eating rat food. The stuff they put out to kill the rats. In the basement. I read it in the paper."

"Did it bite anybody?"

"No. But the rat food didn't hurt it, it's stronger than a rat much stronger and the rat food didn't affect it, it was in good condition when found, they said."

"Well what about its mate?"

"Well maybe it didn't have a mate. There was nothing in the paper about finding its mate."

"So its mate is probably lurking around the Cloisters waiting to bite someone."

"Probably no one will go to the Cloisters until they find its mate."

"Maybe it didn't have a mate. Maybe it was a bachelor or something."

"Well you can't just assume that."

"Maybe it was *seeking* its mate. That got lost in the vast basements of the Cloisters."

"I don't know why you have to romanticize a rabid skunk."

"I was just thinking."

"He's indifferent."

"I don't think he's indifferent. He fucks well enough. Not the best I've ever seen."

104

14

"He can't tell us apart."

"Oh I don't think that's true. He asked me when my birthday was."

"What'd you tell him?"

"I told him. July third."

"Well what does that prove?"

"He's thoughtful. He can tell one from another. He's interested in us as individuals."

"Maybe it's just a façade. Maybe he just knows what to do to make us think he cares about us as individuals and is doing it."

"Why would he do that? If he cares about us as individuals?"

"Because he likes us to have the feeling that he cares about us as individuals? Because it makes things more warm?"

"Well if he wants to make things more warm I'd say that was something in his favor."

"Yes but you have to make a distinction between making things seem a certain way and having them really be a certain way."

"Well even if he's only interested in making things seem a certain way that means he's not indifferent. To the degree that he makes the effort."

"That's true."

"But maybe, on the other hand, he really cares. About us as individuals."

"How would we know?"

"There would be little touches, little individual touches—"

"Like what?"

"Well when I fuck a guy, when he's inside me, I have this little individual thing I do, I don't know how to describe it, it's a kind of hooking motion, it, by it I mean the vagina, grabs the penis around the throat, what you might call the throat, at a certain point, a kind of choking, and then it lets go and then it does it again."

"Well what about it?"

"Well he noticed."

"Well I have some things I know how to do too."

"Like what?"

"Well that's my business isn't it? I don't necessarily have to go around explaining my techniques."

"Well I think we're putting this thing too much on a technical basis, that's interesting but it's not the main thing. The main thing is whether he really cares about us on an individual basis."

"How do we find out?"

"Maybe we could give him some sort of a test."

"I don't think Simon is the kind to respond well to a test. It might make him mad."

"Well this is not the only place in the world we can live."

"I know that but how much money do you have?"

"I have a check my grandmother sent for my birthday."

"How much?"

"Twenty-five dollars."

"That'll take us about to the corner."

SIMON was delighted to be fifty-three, lean and aggressive except for his belly which was not lean and aggressive. He was younger than I. M. Pei, younger than Dizzy Gillespie, younger than the Pope. He had more wisdom packed in his little finger than was to be found in the entire Sweets catalog, with its pages of alluring metal moldings and fire-rated expansion joints. He had kept asbestos and asbestos-containing products out of every job he had ever worked on, sometimes at considerable cost. He had a daughter who would come into the kitchen at breakfast and say, "Who's got the goddamn *New York Times*?" Sarah did not wake well. He could spell 49,999 words correctly and make a pretty good stab at many of the rest. He had a Bronze

107

Star, courtesy of a clerk-typist in his unit whose gift for writing citations for routinely rotating personnel had been envied even at Corps level. The IRS regarded him as a cash cow, on a small scale, and regularly sent him loving salutations, including, one year, a box of Godiva chocolates. He could speak persuasively in meetings, maintaining a grave and thoughtful countenance and letting all the dumb guys speak first. He had about twice the élan of youth, normal élan plus extra élan derived from raw need and grain spirits. Several of the male members of his family had lived to be fifty-nine or sixty. "Grow or die" was the maxim that most accorded with his experience and when he did not think of himself as a giraffe he thought of himself as a tree, a palm, schematically a skinny curving vertical with a lot of furor at the top. With colored felt pens and a pad of tracing paper he could produce impressive sketches in twenty minutes, which he then had to reconcile with reality and sweat over for forty days, cursing himself for his facility. "What about the cornstalk?" A design prof had told the students that there were no right angles in nature, and Simon had raised the question of the cornstalk. Had he to do it again, thirty years later, he would have raised the question of the telephone pole, a deterioration of sensibility, perhaps. He rushed toward things, normally, his present quietude a parenthesis in a life not unmarked by strife and contestation. Pipe bombs did not bother him so long as they did not blow his face off. The assassination of the Swedish Prime Minister, on the other hand, scarred his

brain. He had met Palme once, at a conference on the
work of the Greek planner Constantin Doxiodes in
Stockholm in 1972, at which Doxiodes had declared
himself a criminal because he had put human beings
into high-rise buildings. Palme had been a beneficent
presence, a short man who wanted everything to go
well, wanted the world to succeed in good socialist fashion, gay and optimistic. "The deed of a lunatic," the
Swedish police said, Simon feeling despair for human-
kind. A friend, a Polish architect who had been at Penn
with him, visited him in Philadelphia in 1984 on a
grant from the Ford Foundation. Carol had made osso
buco and they had talked for hours. "Socialism, finally,
doesn't work," Ryszard had said. "You get, you know,
too many bad guys at the top." Ryszard's father had
been a deputy in the Polish parliament, a Communist
who sat for some years and had then been jailed follow-
ing a change in the leadership. It was the first time that
anyone had said to Simon, with the authority of three
decades of involvement, that socialism *didn't work.*
"You get, at the summit, not the worst but the next-
worst." Simon took Ryszard to the airport, gave him as
a going-away present a Tizio lamp, regretted that he
saw him so seldom, wished that he lived next door, on
Pine Street. Carol, when they were twenty-five and
twenty-six, had been a smart-ass, an admirable smart-
ass. "I love you but it's only temporary," she had said.
She was fond of saying to people, "Here's wishing you a
happy and successful first marriage." Simon could lift
refrigerators other people couldn't lift. He had almost

crushed his left hand getting a refrigerator down a set of right-angled stairs for a neighbor. His muscles responded brightly to challenge. Fifty-three, he thought, was not so much worse than twenty-three. All giraffes think this.

"H E used a rolled-up newspaper," Veronica says, "what you'd use on a dog. Only he put his back into it, when I was twelve and thirteen and fourteen. What can I say? Sadistic son-of-a-bitch. If he'd been a drunk I could maybe have forgiven him but he didn't drink. He was a piano salesman, worked for this piano store downtown. He played pretty well himself. He'd wanted to be a doctor. My mother got rid of him, eventually. Not soon enough."

Simon thinks of his own large, calm father, still active at seventy-five, playing the market and raising hell on behalf of the ADA. She's wearing patched jeans (patches at the back of the knee, just under a buttock, on the right thigh) and a dead-black sweater. Blond hair done in cornrows this morning, a copy of *Interview* in her lap, somebody named Kim Basinger on the cover. He wants to hold her tight, rock her, even—a non-rational impulse, she's almost as tall as he is.

"Well, it's a bitch," he says. This sounds feeble even to him.

"He looked nice in a suit. He had these pretty expensive suits, maybe a dozen suits. He had a lot of shoes, I remember the shoes with shoetrees in them. He gave me a very good camera when I was fifteen, a Mamiyaflex, a twin-lens reflex. I used to take pictures of lizards, lizard-on-branch, lizard-on-brick-wall, lizard looking at camera—"

"And your mother?"

"She was kind of a dishrag, to tell the truth. Then. She pulled her socks up after she got rid of him. She's still back there, in Denver. She's a school principal, elementary school. Got a boyfriend, the shop teacher. She thinks she's doing *Lady Chatterley's Lover.*"

She pauses.

"Guess what," she says.

"What?"

"You're not a father-figure. That surprise you?"

"No."

"You're more like a guy who's stayed out in the rain too long."

Does this translate into *experienced, tried-and-true, well-tempered?* Or *pulpy, hanging-in-thin-strips?* He pulls at an ear.

"I mean worn, but with a certain character."

Rust never sleeps, he thinks. "Well," he says, "shall
we take the children to school?"

"What children?"

"Right."

"Are you going to have any more children?"

"Probably not."

TIM, the professional whistler, is a sad Saab of a man about thirty. He has appeared on a number of local tv shows and plays club dates occasionally. He whistles "Twilight Time," "Tumbling Tumbleweeds," and "My Blue Heaven," the latter taken note-for-note from the famous record by Gene Austin. His whistling is tough, very tough, with many complicated flourishes. Tim says that the most famous whistler of all time was Fred Lowry, who whistled for both Vincent Lopez and Horace Heidt and His Musical Knights. The version of the "William Tell Overture" Lowry did with Heidt has never been surpassed, Tim says.

After dinner (roasted squab with chicken-fried potato skins) Tim talks additionally about whistling. Dore

114

PARADISE

is moving nervously between the kitchen and the sitting room. Fred Lowry's version of "Indian Love Call" sold more than two million copies, Tim tells them. He himself has had several careers other than whistling, notably high-tech electronics in California.

"I had this place in Mountain View. I had everything, projection television, walk-around no-hands telephones, stereo, a Nautilus machine, whirlpool bath, two BMWs, two dogs, PC with printer, shotguns, lots of shotguns, handguns, Alvar Aalto chairs and tables and chaises, art, some very fine art, three Diebenkorns, two Clementes, the house was by Frank Gehry, great trees, wine cellar, great California wines, I used to go around to the vineyards for the tastings, got to know a lot of the growers, thirty suits, this one is by Issey Miyake, he did it especially for me—"

"Any of this true?" Veronica whispers.

"How would I know?" Simon whispers.

Tim is drinking Black Russians. Simon has gone out to obtain Kahlua and brandy.

"What we were basically doing," Tim says, "was voice synthesis. The first application is clearly for people who've lost their voices because of operations or one thing and another. Then toys, vending machines, voiceprint applications for banking and of course the whole telecommunications thing. Bell Labs is heavily, heavily into this but we were doing some things that would have scared them if they'd known."

Dore looks at Simon. Simon inclines his head to the left, meaning *Could be.*

"Digital is unbelievable," Tim says. "I can take an ordinary utterance and give it a nasty sneering tone, just by bending some numbers. I can—"

Veronica says, "So what are you doing now?"

"Car wash," Tim says, "over on Tenth Avenue. Washing cars. What most people don't know is that the finish on today's cars, especially the Japanese cars, actually *embraces* the dirt. I mean if you wanted the dirt to adhere to the finish you couldn't come up with a better . . . There are these tiny pits uniformly distributed over the surface of the car that act like traps for the grime, reach out and suck it up. It becomes like plaque on teeth. Now, you wonder why they can't devise a solvent that would dissolve the plaque and not harm the enamel. I'm telling you, the formula exists. It is *in being*. But because the big dentifrice outfits don't want to lose a very, very lucrative market, you and I get zip. Have to go in twice a year and have some dental assistant scrape away with the old hand tool for an hour. Are you familiar with the work of Buckminster Fuller? Have you read what Fuller has to say about copper wire? The earth's supply of copper is finite. Our per capita investment in copper, for every man, woman and child on earth—"

Simon's getting tired. "But of course you can look at it in another way," he says.

"Look at what?"

"The whole thing. The deficit. The government is the biggest consumer in the country, right? And that's going to be true by and large of all governments everywhere. So if every government contract were tied to a

116

proportionate amount which would go to reduction of the deficit, if you couldn't get government work without—"

"They'd just cost-plus you," says Tim.

"No more cost-plus," Simon says. "We've done away with it."

"They'd just bury it somewhere else."

"More auditors."

"Banks wouldn't give you your capitalization."

"Nationalize 'em."

"You want an across-the-board standardization of profit? Where do you get your incentive?"

"Say three tiers of incentive tied to productivity. So there'd be a meaningful variation but not flat-out rape, if you know what I mean."

Tim sighs and strips off his jacket. "I once heard Fuller speak for seven straight hours. I only understood a tenth of what he was saying. By the end of the evening there were only five people left in the audience. He'd started with three hundred. I went home and began to make tetrahedrons with Play-Doh and toothpicks at two o'clock in the morning. What would the three tiers be?"

"Say the prime rate is six, one, two and three times the prime rate. To get eighteen you'd have to do awfully good work."

"Who decides?"

"Be the reverse of cost-plus. The multiplier would be how much ahead of time and how much under budget."

"Underneath the paint, God knows what."

"Our inspectors would take sections."

Tim says, "That's terribly rational, Simon. The idea of progress is philosophically dubious, you know that."

"Not talking about progress. Talking about movement. We're not necessarily married to the present situation."

Tim looks at the three women.

"Too bad. Engineering is key. We haven't even floated the subject of smoking. Every day, fifteen to twenty Americans are injured by their ashtrays."

SIMON enjoyed life as a ghost, one of the rewards of living in the great city. So many units rushing to and fro that nobody noticed anything much or had time to remark on strangers in the house, in the neighborhood. Sublets were everywhere, two men and a grand piano might pop up in your building any Wednesday. Maybe old blockwatchers of thirty years' standing were keeping running censuses of the population, but Simon did not know the old blockwatchers and so felt comfortably anonymous. For amusement, he cooked, or went to a neighborhood movie. He saw *The Benny Goodman Story* and *Silverado,* the first with Anne and the second with Dore and Veronica. Dore and Veronica had not heard of Benny Goodman and thus weren't interested; Anne didn't like Westerns. "How can you not like Westerns?" Simon asked her, truly amazed, and she had said that when she was a child she had seen one in which Indians had tied a man to two bent-down saplings and then cut a rope and the saplings had rent the man into two distinct pieces and that she had never seen a Western since. Simon told her that not all Westerns had that kind of thing in them but she remained unpersuaded. Simon read, much of the time, and consulted with them on their plans.

The first plan was to return to Denver, and nobody liked it. "Be damned if I will," Veronica had said, and Anne had said the same thing. The second plan was to go to Paris and affiliate themselves with one of the couture houses there, Saint-Laurent or Karl Lagerfeld. Although the best stuff was coming from Milan, they said. They talked knowledgeably about Memphis, at least the fabrics. The third plan was to join the Army and acquire training in a number of sophisticated electronic and computer skills. The fourth plan was Burger King.

"A lot of Americans work at Burger King. On a contingency basis."

"Americans of every creed and stripe."

"I'd rather go to Harvard?"

"Transferring one-and-a-half ragged years at Fort Lupton Community?"

"Yeah, yeah, I know."

"I want to write music."

"What kind of music?"

"Serious music. Big music. Entire string sections bending to the work."

"You could study that."

"I could. Where is this Juilliard place?"

"I think you have to play something before you can get in."

"Tambourine? Naw that's a joke I know tambourine is no good."

"Do you think we started too late?"

"It's never too late. In principle."

"Chase has a plan for bank tellers."

"I don't want to be a bank teller."

"Well it's a start."

"Toward what?"

"I don't want to think we're fucked. I really don't want to think that."

"We could go out and marry some more people."

"The last thing I have in mind."

"Yeah it does sound a little retrograde."

Anne is in a retrospective mood.

"I won the Colorado Miss Breck," she says. "I didn't win the National, though."

"Can't win 'em all," Simon says.

"It was very exciting. This stuff is very exciting when you're a kid, people making a fuss over you. It becomes less exciting. I wanted to be a doctor."

"Everybody wants to be a doctor. Veronica's old man the child-beater wanted to be a doctor."

"I know," she says. "Helping people. Your existence is justified."

Simon looks at his khakis; they're a bit on the filthy

121

side. Buy another pair. "You could still do that," he says. "Medical school."

"Do you want to get married again?"

"Hadn't thought about it."

"Probably somebody'd marry you."

"Like who?"

"Some dumb woman. A commodity with which the world is amply supplied. Me, for example."

"That would be pretty dumb. You need a young soldier."

"You telling me what I need?"

"Trying to."

"I feel affectionate toward you, Simon."

"I feel the same thing. Not a good idea."

"Who says?"

"Aetna Life and Casualty."

VERONICA is missing. Not precisely missing, absent, rather. For several days nobody mentions the fact. Then on a Monday Anne says, "I wonder where the hell Veronica is."

"Probably with Thag," Dore says.

"Thag? Who is Thag?" Simon asks.

"Guy she met at the laundromat," Anne says. "He's a broker. He's with Smith Barney."

"If he's a broker what's he doing at the laundromat?"

"So he's thrifty. She should have called, though."

"Probably having a great time. The time of her life," says Dore. "They're probably sitting there drinking Dom Pérignon and buying and selling Carbide right

123

now." Dore reads the financial pages of the newspapers carefully and has fifty shares in a concern that is marketing a corrective for dry eye, or the inability to tear, a painful and depressing condition that afflicts hundreds of thousands of Americans and countless foreigners, she says.

"What kind of a name is Thag?" Simon asks irritably.

"I think it's a beautiful name," Dore says. "Very Scandinavian."

"Well if she doesn't get her ass back here pretty damn quick I'm going to give her bed away."

"Simon!" Anne exclaims. "You're being possessive!"

"I don't mean it."

"I know. That's the hell of it."

"You don't want me to be possessive."

On the street Simon and Anne gaze at a brand-new Honda, the paint a glittering candy red.

"I don't like what Honda did with the front end this year," he says.

"Yeah, it's insensitive."

Simon makes a shaping gesture with his hand.

"That snout."

Anne nods.

"Very wrong. Still—" He puts an arm around her. "The first car I ever bought was a Hillman Minx. Ever see one of those?"

"Before my time," she says.

"A boxy little ragtop. Had all the power of a lawnmower. Never had a car after that I liked as much."

"During which marriage was that?"

"You getting on me?"

"Not me."

"And I was going to take us for oysters at the Oyster Bar."

"I'm ready."

"A certain dryness sets in. The situation dries out, as it were."

"I didn't mean to pry."

"When I was young I thought everything was very funny. I cracked up a lot. Don't do that anymore."

"Youthful arrogance."

"I'd still like to think everything was funny."

"I used to work with children," Anne says.

"Disturbed children?"

"Not more disturbed than any other children. Just ordinary children."

"What did you do?"

"I worked with them. We worked together, me and the children."

"Can you be more specific?"

"I just worked with them. Ordinary children. The children need a lot of work. They're just like anybody else. They need a lot of work. They're not finished. We glued things to paper plates. I worked with them. Daily. On a daily basis."

"You had a place where you worked with them?"

"Yeah it was a kind of nursery. Painted greige. Gray-beige. The color is thought to have a bearing on how the children feel. Some places have a lot of bright colors, that's another theory, this was a soothing calming color. Greige."

"So what were the children like?"

"You can't generalize, they were all different. Not every child feels the same thing at the same time. They were all different. For example, some of them were male."

At the Oyster Bar under Grand Central they sit at a table next to four men in business suits. One of the men has no arms and has removed his shoes. He has mittenlike socks on his feet and holds, between the big toe and the next of the right foot, what looks to Simon like a Gibson.

Q: You must be tired. Fatigued.

A: No I'm not a bit tired.

Q: All of that . . . activity must have left you a bit tired.

A: Yes I suppose you could think that.

Q: You're not tired.

A: You mean mentally tired?

Q: Physically.

A: No I'm not tired. I feel fine.

Q: How are the headaches?

A: Haven't been having them.

Q: That doesn't mean they won't come back.

A: The aspirin did the job.

Q: It wasn't aspirin it was Tylenol. Extra-Strength Tylenol.

A: Did the job.

Q: Yes it's supposed to be quite good. The drug houses send people around, detail men, they leave me samples of all sorts of things, I give them to patients. Free.

A: That's extremely generous.

Q: Well otherwise they'd just rot, wouldn't they? I mean I have buckets and buckets. All brightly colored.

A: I assume you don't drink. Except in moderation.

Q: Also, I've given up smoking. It was quite a battle. The second finger on my right hand used to be brown, a yellow-brown. Now it's not.

A: You feel better.

Q: I feel a little less stupid. So you were pretty much in hog heaven, there, with the three women, for all those months . . .

A: As a situation, as a domestic situation, it was not unstressful. There were, naturally, competing interests, people whose interests at any one time were not congruent—

Q: You mean they fought.

A: They were sisterly most of the time. Once in a while they fought.

Q: Using what means?

A: Mouth, mostly.

Q: Not laceration of the skin by fingernails, hair-tearing, bosom-bashing . . .

A: None of that. They were, most of the time, very good to one another.

Q: Remarkable.

A: I thought so.

Q: When I was first married, when I was twenty, I didn't know where the clitoris was. I didn't know there was such a thing. Shouldn't somebody have told me?

A: Perhaps your wife?

Q: Of course she was too shy. In those days people didn't go around saying, This is the clitoris and this is what its proper function is and this is what you can do to help out. I finally found it. In a book.

A: German?

Q: Dutch.

DORE sitting in the back of the house, watching a bird-fight. Two black birds are struggling in midair near the ailanthus.

"That one sucker is going to get the other sucker," she says. "Going to clean his clock for him."

"That's the way it is in this world," says Tim. "What does he win if he wins?"

"Don't know."

"You think Simon's been all right lately?"

"Morose," she says. "I get a definite moroseness."

"Yeah. That's kind of what I was talking about. Some people can't stand prosperity."

"You think he wants to go back to Philadelphia?"

"He hasn't said yea or nay. I gather things weren't so wonderful in Philadelphia."

"Where did you go to school?"

"Cornell."

"What did you study?"

"Electrical engineering."

"Is that a good place for it?"

"It's okay."

"What's your wife's name?"

"Carol."

"Everybody's wife is named Carol. You ever notice that?"

"I didn't know that, no."

"Is she pretty?"

"No. Maybe kind of."

"Oh. What's she like?"

"I can see her in long red robes with a little red yar-mulke on her head and a big gold cross on a chain around her neck and a ring that you have to kiss. Standing just to the left of the throne and whispering into the ear of the king."

"Is that Machiavelli?"

"I was thinking more of that guy who worked for Nixon."

"What does she think of you?"

"Not much. I work at the car wash, remember?"

"But that's only temporary."

"By me everything's temporary. Good things and bad things."

"That must be fascinating. The indeterminacy."

"It's fascinating."

HE lost nine pounds (a great blessing) during the eight months they lived in the apartment. They had not been slow to criticize his toes, teeth, belly, hair, or politics. "It seems to me," Veronica had said one day, "that you have no social responsibility." "My first social responsibility," he had said, "is that the building doesn't collapse." "Right right right," she said, "but you are after all a creature of the power structure. You work for the power structure." This was true enough, revolutionaries didn't build buildings, needed only closets to oil their Uzis in, no work for architects there. On the other hand Veronica and the others derived their own politics from a K-Mart of sources, Thomas Aquinas marching shoulder-to-shoulder with Simone de Beauvoir and the weatherbeaten troopers of *Sixty Minutes*. They were often left and right during the same conversation, sometimes the same sentence.

His headaches had gone away but had been replaced by early-morning vomiting. A few ounces of yellow bile produced each morning. He meditated on *too much*, thought carefully about *a sufficiency*. When the women had been living with him he had thought of himself, very often, as insufficiently virile, or insufficiently ambitious. Who needed this much excitation? On the other hand, who could resist it? Anne sometimes looked like a twenty-year-old, especially when she'd just bathed, the small breasts, the small hips, the dark hair. Dore was tall and bossy, there was no other word for it, and Veronica was, take your choice, sassy or critical, great lip on that kid, never without a spiked remark. He had the sense that he was a hotel, didn't mind being a hotel, okay I'm a hotel. Two of them sucking his cock in the early mornings, taking turns, five or six o'clock, he was drinking white wine, not very good white wine, and smoking, this went on for a long while, sometimes they'd turn to one another and one would begin to lick the inside of the other's legs up near the cunt, quite near, Simon with his hands on that one's buttocks, around her waist and then moving down over the buttocks with slow appreciative strokes, raking them with his nails at intervals, but softly, little bites, but softly, the flesh is so delicious Dore said, or Anne said.

"Y OU'VE been bad Veronica."

"No I haven't that's not bad that's hardly bad at all."

"I agree with her. You've been bad."

"No I haven't I don't call that—"

"Very bad."

"I don't call that bad that's not hardly bad at all you should see what I've seen if you want to talk about—"

"Yes Veronica yes of course of course Veronica I didn't think you'd admit it why should you? C'mon Anne there's no reasoning with her."

"Dore don't go I haven't been bad she's just trying to tell you I've been bad but I mean are you going to believe her? Just because she says—"

"Well how do you feel?"

134

"Bad."

"You see."

"Oh God Dore now you've made her feel bad just talking about everything you've made her feel bad that she's done something some little something she shouldn't have done some little something that warrants horrible contrition—"

"I don't mind making her feel bad. She's bad."

"Veronica, are you essentially what she says you are? Bad? You can tell me I'm your friend. I have other bad friends, if that—"

"Well spit. That's what I think."

"You're not going to talk is that it?"

"Hit her."

"I'm not going to hit her she's a sister you can't hit a sister even a bad sister that's one of the eternal rules not even a terribly, terribly bad sister. Like Veronica."

"I'm about as bad as I want to be, so far. I haven't thought about haven't grasped how bad I might want to be in the future when my ship comes in or something. Something, then, may be released in me that will allow—"

"I don't think she's going to acknowledge the clear facts. I don't think she has the humility. I give up I absolutely give up."

"Hang me if you want to I don't care. Where's the rope? Get the rope. Hang me."

"Oh hit her go ahead and hit her I can't stand this mewling."

"I don't *want* to hit her."

"Hit me."

"Hit her."

"What with?"

"God I don't know use your fist kick her what do I care it's not my problem is it. Hit her."

"You don't think that's a little severe?"

"It's gonna take a goddamn presidential order to get you to hit her?"

"Why me?"

"Okay I've been bad. I admit it. But others have been worse. I could point some fingers."

"Lord I'm tired of listening to this drivel if you don't get it together in the next three to five minutes I'm going to—"

"What?"

S IMON'S father died and he flew back to California for the funeral. He had to buy a dark suit, went to Barney's and picked the first one that seemed to fit him. In San Francisco he stood next to his mother, their arms entwined, while the Presbyterian minister said what he could. The chapel was empty except for the two of them and an elderly couple his mother had introduced as Connie and Bill and who turned out to be golfers, part of a mixed foursome his father had played with once a week. The other woman was unable to be present because of a daughter giving birth in Corvallis, Oregon. His mother didn't play.

Afterward, back at her handsome Pacific Heights house, his mother said: "What are you doing?"

137

"Taking a little time off."

"It's been months now."

"Excellent months."

"Just asking."

"What's the money situation?"

"Your father was very good about that, as you know. That Carbide he bought years ago at twelve? He sold it just before he died at seventy-three. When they were having that trouble. He had almost ten thousand shares. Actually it went up to seventy-eight last week but he did very well, very well. We have some other stuff that's looking good."

"How about coming to New York? I have a place you'd like. Needs furniture. We could go out and buy a lot of furniture."

"I don't want to buy any more furniture," his mother said. "I like it here. I'll have to see how it feels. If I need you I'll call you, rely on it."

"Nothing more fun than buying furniture."

"I agree. But it has to be going toward something."

Nothing to say to that.

His father had been a lumberman, a prophet of redwood. Redwood was light, easily milled, plentiful, took a stain well, weathered beautifully. Tens of hundreds of thousands of board feet of California redwood had passed through the family's logging and milling operations, his father not the biggest lumberman in the state but not the smallest. Simon remembered odd moments: putting a huge dollop of Worcestershire sauce on a hamburger in a restaurant and his father telling him, "Don't do that, son, it whips up the body." Sitting by the radio in 1938 listening to the second Louis-Schmeling fight, sitting by the radio all night long in 1939 listening to accounts of the German invasion of Poland. When Simon had been expelled from USC, before he went to Penn, he had come home and told his father about it, and his father's only comment was, "What are we going to tell your mother?" The death of the father is supposed to release a burst of new creative energy, he remembered. He felt nothing but sadness and admiration.

Back in New York he receives a notice for jury duty. How can this be? He's not registered to vote. Nevertheless he dutifully hauls himself down to 60 Centre Street one Monday morning. The benches on the fifteenth floor of the Criminal Courts Building are filled with readers. He spots at least twenty paperback copies of le Carré's *The Little Drummer Girl*, which he himself has read and greatly enjoyed. He falls into conversation with a young woman who is, he learns, the editor of a trade journal dealing with lingerie. She's knitting furiously, a sleeveless sweater, as she talks. "We make nine hundred thousand a year for the company, profit," she says. "Can you believe it?" She produces fourteen issues a year, with each issue running to ninety-six pages of editorial and God knows how many of ads. "It's hard to think of things to feature after a while," she confesses. "How many ways of bifurcating breasts are there? We take a lot of clues from the artists. Memphis is in now, spatter and clatter."

139

The lingerie editor tells him that her assistant is a berserko and that it's impossible to get good subordinates these days. Simon, empaneled, is knocked off a murder case, empaneled again, is knocked off a rape case. "The defendant is accused of sexual misconduct," the blond woman judge tells the jurors. "Will the defendant stand up so that the jurors can see him?" The defendant stands and almost involuntarily takes a little bow. When the attorneys, questioning Simon in the jury box, ask him what he is, he says he is an architect. At the lunch break on the third day, he meets, in a cluster of fast food stands in a little park near the courthouses, a red-haired woman who says she is a poet.

THE three women looked for jobs but were turned down by Bendel, Bergdorf, Bloomingdale's, Lord & Taylor, Charles Jourdan, Ungaro, Altman's, Saks, Macy's. They tried all the modeling agencies, starting with Ford and working their way down the list. Simon designed and had printed composites for them and they left these at every ad agency of any size in the city. They applied for substitute teacher positions but found this a closed shop, they needed New York State credentials which they didn't have. In a moment of desperation they filed applications for the Fire Department but were told they were so far down on the list that they had no reasonable hope of consideration before 1999, when they would be too old to begin training.

141

Anne and Veronica are fighting.

"Stupid bitch!"

"Asshole!"

"C'mon, guys," Simon says. "What's the deal?"

"She's a motherfucker and a dumb motherfucker," Anne says. "Crummy cheapo slut."

"Look who's talking," Veronica says, jumping out of Anne's reach. "Miss Cunt of 1986."

"What's this about? What's the issue?"

"Simon you're so fucking reasonable," Veronica says, sitting down on the couch.

"I say, what's going on?"

"She got us a job," Anne says.

"Terrific," says Simon. "What's the job?"

"Convention. The National Sprinkler Association. At the Americana. We have to stand under these things and get sprinkled. I won't do it."

"What if they gave us raincoats?"

"It's not raincoats they want to see."

"What if I said transparent plastic raincoats?"

"I might do it with transparent plastic raincoats."

"I'll call the guy and see what he says. It's two hundred each."

"Raincoats and body stockings."

"No thrill in body stockings."

"Let them use their vile imaginations."

"I just feel like a body."

"What in God's name do you think they want?"

"I know, I know."

"Look at it this way," Simon says. "A body is a gift. A great body is a great gift."

"All I need. A Unitarian minister."

"You don't have to take the job."

"*We don't have any money.*"

"You want me to make a little pile of money and burn it right here on the floor? There's enough money around. Take it easy. Wait until you find something you want."

"We're concubines."

"You can make everything sound as terrible as you want," Simon says. "I'm going to bed."

"Who with?"

Simon's wife's lawyer's letter arrives and outlines her demands: She wants full custody of the child, the Pine Street house, both cars, sixty-five thousand dollars a year in alimony, child support at a level consonant with the child's previous style of life, fifty percent of all retirement funds, IRA, Keogh and the firm's, fifty percent of his partnership interest in the firm in perpetuity, and fifty percent of all odds and ends of stocks, bonds, cash and real property not subsumable under one of the previous rubrics. The client has been severely damaged in all ways by Simon's desertion and the years of fiendish abuse that had preceded it, the letter suggests.

"What are you going to do?" Veronica asks.

"Give it to her, I guess."

"Were you really that bad?"

"He may be overstating it a bit."

"We are *pure skin.*"

SIMON meets the poet at the International Arrivals Building, holding one hand behind him. The nine-hour Finnair flight from Helsinki has been exhausting, but she has met A, B, C, and D—Russian poets so fabulously gifted that none of them has been allowed to publish so much as a weather report. "That's terrific," he says. "You look beautiful." "They all speak English," she says, "this half-misunderstood English which is three times as good as regular English." She notices that he is holding something behind his back. "What's that?" He produces a large, naked steak, a steak big as a Sunday *Times*. She is embarrassed and pops the steak into her canvas carryall. "I don't get your metaphor," she says in the cab. "Is it hunger?"

She's right, it is hunger. Don't tell her.

They sit in her kitchen. "The burning barns in your poems," he says, "why so many? Isn't that a little . . . repetitive?" "My burning barns," she says, "my splendid burning barns, I'll burn as many barns as I damn please, Pappy." He is older than she is, by ten years, and she has given him this not altogether welcome nickname. She looks absolutely stunning, a black three-quarter-length skirt embossed with black bird figures, a knitted sleeveless jacket, a yellow long-sleeved blouse, a red ascot. "Seriously, do you think there are too many? Barns?" It's the first time she has asked his opinion about anything connected with her work. "I was half teasing," he says. "But they did burn," she says. "Every one I've ever known." "Simon says," Simon says, "Simon needs a beer." She rises and moves to fetch a St. Pauli Girl from the refrigerator.

The poet lives in the country, in an old Putnam County farmhouse that she has not touched except to paint the walls pale blue. She has painted over the old wallpaper, and the walls puff and wrinkle in places. The furniture is junk golden oak, one piece to a room except in the kitchen, where there is a table and two mismatched chairs. "This one is Biedermeier," the poet says, "from my mother, and the other, the potato-chip jobbie, is Eames, from my father. That tell you anything?"

Simon takes the train from Grand Central to Putnam County. He doesn't like the train, almost always in miserable repair and without air conditioning, and he hates changing at Croton, the rush from one train to another more like a stampede than anything else, but the views of the stately Hudson from the discolored windows are wonderful, and when he alights at Garrison at the end of this trip she is sitting on the hood of her circus-red Toyota pickup, drinking apple juice from a paper cup.

The poet sings to him:

> Row, row, row your bed
> Gently down the stream . . .

THE professional whistler's wife calls and says that if the resident bitches and tarts don't keep their hands off her husband she will cause a tragic happenstance.

"Sounded a little pissed," Anne says.

"These housewives," says Veronica, "I guess you can't blame them they don't have the latitude."

Dore says, "Let her come around, her ass is grass."

"Simon is passive."

"I don't think he's so passive he grasps you very tightly. I think the quality of the embrace is important."

"I think he's more active than passive. I'm still sore. I don't call that passive."

147

"He's at a strange place in his life."

"You're like one of those people who have tiny little insights of no consequence."

"The hell you say."

"You're like one of those people who have weird figurative growths on their minds that come out in dismal exfoliations."

"You're funnin' me."

"You're like one of those people who don't know their ass from their elbow."

"Well there's no need to be vulgar."

"Yes there is."

"Who says?"

"I say."

"Well there's no need to be vulgar."

"You want one?"

"One what?"

"Bang."

"What's it got on it?"

"Sprinkles."

"Naw I'm not decadent."

"He's slender."

"You call that slender?"

"I except the paunch."

"He can go maybe eighteen times in a good month."

"That's depressing."

"I think it's depressing."

"I really want to be more vulgar than I am at present being."

"Well who the fuck's stopping you?"

"I guess nobody."

"I guess we could dance cheek-to-cheek."

"I guess we could tear up some little bunches of violets."

"Well there's no need to be destructive."

"We pretend to be okay."

"I'm fine. I'm really fine."

"I was fine. Spent a lot of time on it, buffing the heels with one of those rocks they sell in the drugstore, oiling the carcass with precious oils— Then I found out. How they exploit us and reduce us to nothing. Mere knitters."

"How'd you find out?"

"Read it in a feminist text."

"I heard they're not gonna let us read any more books."

"Where'd you hear that?"

"Just around. On the Rialto."

"Maybe it would be better for us so we wouldn't be so exacerbated."

"You're like one of those people who lay down the flag in the dirt before it's time."

"Well that's what you say you fool."

"I want the car of my dreams."

"What is it?"

"Camaro."

"You're like one of those people who have really shitty dreams, know what I mean? Really shitty dreams."

"How can you say that?"

"I played in a band once."

"What was your instrument?"

"Tambourine."

"Can't get a union card for tambourine."

"My knee all black and blue, I banged my tambourine on it. First the elbow, then the knee."

"I saw a beautiful ass. In a picture. It was white and was walking away from the camera. She was holding hands with a man. He was naked too it was a beautiful picture."

"How'd that make you feel?"

"Inferior."

"Well that's what you say you idiot."

"I'd like to light up a child's life. I apologize I was wrong."

"Yes you were wrong."

"But I still think what I think."

"It's hard to get a scrape when you want to light up a child's life."

"I've done it three times."

"Leaves you heavy of heart."

"It does."

A: I've crossed both major oceans by ship, the Pacific twice, on troopships, the Atlantic once, on a passenger liner. You stand out there, at the rail, at dusk, and the sea is limitless, water in every direction, never-ending, you think *water forever,* the movement of the ship seems slow but also seems inexorable, you feel you will be moving this way forever, the Pacific is about seventy million square miles, about one-third of the earth's surface, the ship might be making twenty knots, I'm eating oranges because that's all I can keep down, twelve days of it with young soldiers all around, half of them seasick— On the Queen Mary, in tourist class, we got rather good food, there was a guy assigned to our table who had known Paderewski, the great pianist

151

who was also Prime Minister of Poland, he talked about Paderewski for four days, an ocean of anecdotes—

Q: I was tempted to become a shrink. But then I decided it wasn't science.

A: But what if she stabs me in the ear with the scissors?

Q: Haven't you realized that she is not going to stab you in the ear with the scissors?

A: A lot of people go along assuming that. And then they get stabbed in the ear with the scissors.

Q: You saw yourself, in relation to the three women, as an artist working in fat.

A: No no no.

Q: I'm a doctor. You can tell me. I'm used to hearing terrible things.

A: I felt blessed.

Q: Your hands are trembling.

A: That happens in the mornings sometimes.

Q: Which one was the best?

A: All lovely, all.

Q: I don't have a clear idea of what these women looked like.

A: Dore had a scar. Right on the cheekbone, parallel to it. A good inch-and-a-half. About as thick as a pencil line, but white. Her hair was what they call ash-blond; she had black eyebrows. Veronica was blond too, a blonder blond. Very good forehead. Wore a ponytail a lot of the time. Anne had dark hair, very long. She had the longest hair.

Q: Did you feel, when you went out on the street with one of them, or to the market, that you looked strange together?

A: Never occurred to me.

Q: You do wear young clothes, youngish wretched clothes, garb of the youth culture slightly misunderstood—

A: Nothing the matter with my clothes. I've always worn these clothes.

Q: You see clients in those clothes?

A: Of course not. I put on a jacket and tie and—

Q: Harris tweed, a blue chambray shirt, dark-red tie of rough wool—

A: It's a uniform, yes.

Q: I'm greatly comforted. I don't like to think of people not wearing their uniforms, out of uniform.

A: Nor do the clients.

Q: Bellies. I've always been greatly drawn to the female belly, as a more subtle, less overt, sculptural representation of all the other tactile values we associate with—

A: All sculpture is about women, if you care to look at it that way. Buildings are about women, cars are about women, landscape is about women, and tombs are about women. If you care to look at it that way. The Grand Canyon.

Q: The Eiffel Tower?

A: About women in the sense of being addressed to women.

Q: Who speaks for the male?

A: Monks.

Q: Is the bicycle about women?

A: Speeds us toward women as twilight time descends and the lamplighters go about their slow incendiary tasks.

Q: What about coveting your neighbor's wife?

A: Well on one side, in Philadelphia, there were no wives, strictly speaking, there were two floors and two male couples, all very nice people. On the other side, Bill and Rachel had the whole house. I like Rachel but I don't covet her. I could covet her, she's covetable, quite lovely and spirited, but in point of fact our relationship is that of neighborliness. I jump-start her car when her battery is dead, she gives me basil from her garden, she's got acres of basil, not literally acres but— Anyhow, I don't think that's much of a problem, coveting your neighbor's wife. Just speaking administratively, I don't see why there's an entire Commandment devoted to it. It's a mental exercise, coveting. To covet is not necessarily to take action.

Q: I covet my neighbor's leaf blower. It has this neat Vari-Flo deal that lets you—

A: I obey the Commandments, the sensible ones. Where they don't know what they're talking about I ignore them. I keep thinking about the story of the two old women in church listening to the priest discoursing on the dynamics of the married state. At the end of the sermon one turns to the other and says, "I wish I knew as little about it as he does."

Q: God critiques us, we critique Him. Does Carol also engage in dalliance?

PARADISE

A: How quaint you are. I think she has friends whom she sees now and again.

Q: How does that make you feel?

A: I wish her well.

Q: What's in your wallet?

A: The usual. Credit cards, pictures of Sarah, driver's license, forty dollars in cash, Amex receipts—

Q: It seems to me that we have quite a great deal to worry about. Does the radish worry about itself in this way? Yet the radish is a living thing. Until it's cooked.

A: Carol is mad for radishes, can't get enough. Rachel gave us radishes, too.

Q: I am feverishly interested in these questions. Ethics has always been where my heart is. Moral precepting stings the dull mind into attentiveness.

A: I'm only a bit depressed, only a bit.

Q: A new arrangement of ideas, based upon the best thinking, would produce a more humane moral order, which we need. Apple honey, disposed upon the sexual parts, is not an index of decadence. Decadence itself is not as bad as it's been painted. As for myself, I am content with too little, I know this about myself and I do not commend myself for it and perhaps one day I shall be able to change myself into a hungrier being, one who acts decisively to grasp—

A: The leaf blower, for example.

THE poet gives him a picture of herself posed naked as a Maja on a couch. The Polaroid is ill-lit, badly composed, unflattering to her stomach, and she is shiny of nose. Furthermore, the couch is ugly, done in inch-square black-and-white hound's-tooth check. "Who took the picture?" Simon asks. "Someone," she says, and snatches it away from him.

He is a layman, not a figure in her world. "You're not a poet, you're a real person," she says. "Of course poets are funnier than real people." She names for his enter- tainment the second, third, fourth, and fifth most beautiful male poets in the country. "But who's the first?" the layman asks. "We keep the position open so that the guys will have something to aspire to," she

156

says. Does she know all of these beautiful poets? Are they all present or former lovers? Simon has no idea how poets behave. *Outrageously* would be his best guess, but what does that mean in practice? The poet's long red hair strays out over the pale-blue pillowcase; her right foot taps time to a Pointer Sisters record. "The dust in your poems," Simon asks, "is it always the same dust? Does it always mean the same thing? Or does it mean one thing in one poem and another thing in another poem?" The poet places a hand under a bare breast, as if to weigh it. "My dust," she says, "my excellent dust. You're a layman, Simon, shut up about my dust."

She was raised in Kansas, where her father is a wholesale grocer. "He gave me this," she says. She opens a book and removes a twenty-thousand-dollar bond. "It was supposed to put me through medical school. I didn't want to go to medical school." The bond is pretty and blue with some kind of noble statuary on it. "Shouldn't this be in a money-market fund or something?" asks the layman. "I guess so," she says. "If you're not from Kansas, people in Kansas ask you: What do you think about Kansas? What do you think about our sky? What do you think about people in Kansas? Are we dumb?" She replaces the bond in the book. "You find a high degree of sadness in Kansas."

"WELL it's just what I thought would happen what I thought would happen and it happened."

"He's a free human individual not bound to us."

"Maybe we're too much for him maybe he needs more of a one-on-one thing see what I'm saying?"

"It may be just a temporary aberration that won't last very long like when suddenly you see somebody in a crowded Pizza Hut or something and you think, I could abide that."

"But if she's a poet then she won't keep him poets burn their candles down to nubs. And then find new candles. That's what they do."

PARADISE

"I don't know I still feel threatened I mean I'm as generous as the next man but I still feel emphatically that our position here has radically altered for the worse. Somehow."

"Poets eat up all of experience and then make poems of it is she any good?"

"He thinks so."

"What does he know he's an architect."

"He was doing Comp Lit before he got kicked out of USC."

"What'd he get kicked out for?"

"Slugged a dean in a riot, it was a First Amendment thing he says."

Tim comes in wearing a dark-blue flannel suit with a faint pinstripe. He leaks prosperity.

"Tim!" Veronica says. "What's happened to you?"

"This is from Paul Stuart," Tim says. "Seven hundred bucks. Do you like it?"

"You look like a new man. A new and better man."

"I got something going," Tim says. "I'm president of this new outfit we're putting together. Medlapse. It's a law firm."

"But you're not a lawyer," Dore says. "Are you?"

"The concept was mine," he says, "lawyers you can Xerox on any street corner. We're specializing in malpractice, it's everywhere. I estimate that forty-seven percent of all patient-physician encounters have elements that would tend to support a successful action. We project a ninety-eight percent rate of recovery over two years."

159

"Veronica's been going to this guy over on Hudson Street," Anne says, "he's kind of peculiar."

"You think he's peculiar I don't think he's peculiar," says Veronica.

"What's . . . " Tim reaching into his jacket for a notebook.

"He insists on being paid in cash only."

"Diddling his taxes."

"He doesn't have a nurse."

"Violation of AMA guidelines on sexual oversight, he's OB-GYN?"

"His name is Linh pronounced Ling he's Vietnamese he was a general in Vietnam."

"They were all generals in Vietnam," Tim says, "what're you seeing him for if you don't mind my asking?"

"Just various things he's cheap, twenty dollars for an office visit."

"When you're ready, Medlapse is ready, can I take you ladies out to lunch, rip up a chop?"

"Where did you have in mind?"

"Blimpie's?"

"You're not going to Blimpie's in that suit?"

"Our cash flow is not on line as yet."

HE'S chopping garlic. Six big cloves of garlic. He minces the garlic and sautés it in olive oil. Meanwhile he's cooking a package of frozen broccoli in a half-cup of salted water. He drains the broccoli and places it in the sauté pan for two or three minutes, at the same time heating a can of chicken broth and half a can of water. He adds chopped parsley to the pan, lets it cook for a bit, then scoops the contents of the sauté pan into the chicken broth and adds a number of slices of hot cooked Italian sausage. He cooks this for a time and then pours it into bowls and adds generous portions of grated parmesan.

A simple soup. Anne says she likes it. "The best soup I've had in decades. I thought I hated broccoli but it just kind of falls apart in this soup and becomes vague green stuff, very tasty. Is it artificially colored?"

"Why do you ask?"

"It's too green."

"That's God's own sun."

"You're sure it's not Union Carbide."

"I don't think Carbide does broccoli."

"This household is a classic case of exploitation by inadversion."

Simon scratches his head like Lionel Barrymore in an old movie. "Tarnation take it," he says, "if I get your drift."

"The male manipulation of every dimension of experience for the suppression and domination of female-kind."

"Right," Simon says. "A big subject."

"Getting bigger every day," she says, suddenly cheerful.

"You see a lot of suppression and domination around here?"

"No this setup doesn't fit the model because it's so laissez-faire. But if we got into its deep structure—" She stops and begins again. "You don't care about anything, Simon. You just go along cooking dinner and fucking us indiscriminately and reading *The Wall Street Journal.* Your vital interests are not involved here. You don't give a shit."

"How do you know?"

Once he'd been in the kitchen with Anne in the early morning. She was wearing a thin transparent shift, nothing else. They had already made love and in the kitchen scuffled for a long time alternately embracing and struggling, Simon running his hands over her breasts, her back, between her legs, Anne hugging him and then jumping up and wrapping her legs around his waist. "This is a female fantasy," she had said, "love in the kitchen." "Love instead of the kitchen," he said, and she said, "But I *like* the kitchen." Her buttocks were such as to drive men wild, drive men wild, he said, and she said that when she'd been in high school she'd worn extremely short shorts with just that in mind, had in fact been sent home a time or two. "My mother couldn't control me," she said, "I was uncontrollable." He picked her up and seated her on top of the refrigerator and she threw an avocado at him and he caught it as it smushed in his hand. He spread her legs and ate her as she sat atop the refrigerator, her arms cradling his head. "Play is what it's all about," she said, "what does it taste like?" "Little bit salty," he said, his tongue laving her belly button, "must be those blackeyed peas we had last night or maybe just your temperament in general."

"So she kicked you out," Anne says.

"She didn't kick me out, exactly."

"Was she better than we are?"

"It was kind of a detour."

"Are you sorry?"

"No."

"It would be nice if you were sorry."

"Everybody always wants somebody to be sorry. Fuck that."

"Veronica had a little thing with a fireman."

"Where'd she get the fireman?"

"A & P. His name was Salvatore. He let her slide down the pole."

"Did he."

"He was married."

"That's tragic. Is it tragic?"

"Just a detour."

He hugs her. "Frolic and detour, the lawyers say."

"But a real poet."

"She's no realer than you are."

"Do you like women more than music?"

"A little."

"You came back because you love us more than you loved her."

"Well, I do."

A: I thought people weren't supposed to have more than three or four nightmares a year. I have them every night, there is no night in which I don't have something that can fairly be described as a nightmare. Many of them have to do with clothes.

Q: The wrong clothes.

A: Not so much the wrong clothes as not being able to get dressed. In particular, the trousers, in dreams I have great, enormous difficulty bringing the trousers up over the knees. The shoes, for some reason I have put on my shoes first and then try to put on the trousers, try to pull them over the shoes . . .

Q: I often dream that my rifle isn't clean. You can clean it and clean it and then the sergeant looks down

the barrel and decides it's not clean, it's got very little
to do with whether the barrel is or is not clean, it's a
metaphysical proposition related to the Art of War,
your poor place within that scheme . . .

A: Every night! It's too much. What recourse? The
grinding of teeth.

Q: Where do you see yourself going from here? In
life.

A: More of the same, I suppose. When I was married
I'd find myself looking forward to *Dumbo*, you know?
Dumbo was going to be on television at say seven-thirty
in the evening and the kid was going to watch it and
that was what I had to look forward to, too.

Q: I liked it.

A: *I* liked it. Bizarre, when you think about it.

Q: The part I remember is when all the storks
dropped all the parachutes from the sky and all the little baby tigers and hippos rolled out of the diapers—
the bundles the storks were carrying were diapers, those
boys don't miss a trick—before the eyes of their astonished tiger and hippo parents. That was cute.

A: Terrifying. Because it was so well done.

Q: I don't want to live on a farm, to go back to the
farm. It's too risky and I don't know what to do. Some
damn cow or other is yelling and I don't know what to
do to alleviate her pain. Do I put the wheat in now or
do I wait two weeks? The combine, its drive chain is
acting up and I ought to be able to fix it by slamming it
a few times with a hammer, but I don't know where to
slam it. I don't know how to talk to the bank. Some

guys know all this stuff and I tell myself I'm not supposed to know it because I'm not a farmer. Yet I think I
ought to be a farmer or at least be capable of being a
farmer. Maybe it's atavistic. . . .

A: I'd be perfectly comfortable living in a hotel. I
take that to be the opposite pole. Not necessarily a
grand hotel, a shabby but still stuffy hotel.

Q: Bedford Square. In London.

A: Never been to London.

Q: Where have you been?

A: Tokyo, Mexico City, Paris, Barcelona, Stockholm, Palermo, Reykjavik—

Q: Lots of hotels in those places.

A: Stayed in the poorer ones, for the most part. Said
to the chambermaid, your breasts look beautiful this
morning.

Q: Shouldn't make fun of them.

A: I wasn't. I lusted after the chambermaids. Not
every one.

Q: Nothing wrong with that.

A: But what if they stab me in the ear with the
feather duster?

Q: Would you like to try some of these little yellow
guys here?

SIMON was a way station, a bed-and-breakfast, a youth hostel, a staging area, a C-141 with the jumpers of the 82nd Airborne lined up at the door. There was no place in the world for these women whom he loved, no good place. They could join the underemployed half-crazed demi-poor, or they could be wives, those were the choices. The universities offered another path but one they were not likely to take. The universities were something Simon believed in (of course! he was a beneficiary) but there was among the women an animus toward the process that would probably never be overcome, not only impatience but a real loathing, whose source he did not really understand. Veronica told him that she had flunked Freshman

168

English 1303 three times. "How in the world did you do that?" he asked. "Comma splices," she said. "Also, every time I wrote down something I thought, the small-section teacher said that it was banal. It probably was banal." Simon found what the women had to say anything but banal, instead edged and immediate. Maybe nothing that could be rendered in a 500-word theme, one bright notion and four hundred and fifty words of hay. Or psychology: *Harlow, rhesus monkeys, raisins, reward.* People did master this stuff, more or less, and emerged more or less enriched thereby. *Compare and contrast extrinsic and intrinsic motivation, giving examples of each.* Father-beaten young women considering extrinsic and intrinsic motivation. "We all went through this," he told them, and Dore said, "Yeah, and you smart guys did the Vietnam war." Simon had opposed the Vietnam war in all possible ways short of self-immolation but could not deny that it was a war constructed by people who had labored through *Psychology I, II, III,* and *IV* and *Main Currents of Western Thought.* "But, dummy, it's the only thing you've got," he said. "Your best idea." "I have the highest respect for education," she said. "The highest. I'd be just as dreary when I came out as I was when I went in."

Howls from outside the front windows. It's past midnight. Simon goes down the stairs to the street.

A man in an old Army field jacket is screaming something about the Supreme Court. He's been screaming, up and down the block, for the past six months. He has

169

an exceptionally deep voice and projects with an actor's
skill. Simon has learned from other people in the
neighborhood that he's called Hal and sleeps on a grate
in front of the hospital.

"Chickenfuckers!" Hal screams.

"Hal," Simon calls.

"Kissass mother!"

"Hal," Simon calls again. "Take this five bucks. Go
eat something."

Hal approaches. He's taller than Simon, about forty,
and wearing a zippered jump suit under the field jacket.

"Up your giggy fuckface," he screams, but a quieter
scream.

"Time for breakfast, Hal."

"Thank you," Hal says in a normal conversational
tone, and takes the bill.

He wheels and marches off down the street, screaming *"Cunts cunts cunts cunts cunts!"*

Simon goes back upstairs.

Veronica comes into his room looking very gloomy.

"We have to talk," she says. She's wearing a rather
sedate dark-blue nightgown, one he hasn't seen before.

"What's the matter?"

"Dore. She's falling apart."

"In what way?"

"She's lost her joy of life."

"I hadn't noticed."

"She tries to hide it from you."

"Maybe it's just temporary."

"I've never seen her like this. She's been reading terrible books. Books about how terrible men are and how they've kept us down."

"That should make her feel better, not worse. I mean, knowing the causes."

"Don't need your cheapo irony, Simon. She's very upset."

"What do you want me to do?"

"Talk to her."

"What can I say? I agree with half that stuff and think the other half is garbage."

"Well it's not for you to decide, is it? Whenever we say something you don't like you say we're hysterical or crazy."

"Me?"

"Men in general."

"Have I ever said you were hysterical or crazy?"

"Probably you didn't want to stir us up. Probably you were thinking it and were just too tactful to say it."

"Are you sure it's Dore who's got this problem?"

"She's been lending us the books. What else do we have to do with our time?"

"So you're all upset."

"The truth shall make you free."

"What makes you think this stuff is the truth?"

"Thirty-five percent of all American women aren't allowed to talk at dinner parties. Think about that."

"How do you know?"

"It's in a book."

In hog heaven the hogs wait in line for more heaven. No, not right, no waiting in line, it's unheavenly, unhogly. The celestial sty is quilted in kale, beloved of hogs. A male hog walks up to a female hog, says "Want to get something going?" She is repulsed by his language, says "Bro, unless you can phrase that better, you're chilly forever." No, that's not right, this is hog heaven, they fall into each other's trotters, nothing can be done wrong here, nothing wrong can be done. . . .

"AHA!" Simon says.

"Not too bad," says Veronica.

"I'll have another," Ralph says. He puts a ten on the bar.

"Me too," says Veronica.

"I'll go along," Simon says.

"You two getting it on, or what?" Ralph asks.

"Just acquaintances," Veronica says. "Mere acquaintances."

"Don't look like mere acquaintances to me," Ralph says. "I have a feel for that sort of thing. There's a way people look. They kind of lean toward each other."

"This music is a little muddy," Simon says. The jukebox is playing a Madonna number, "Into the Groove."

173

"You mean conceptually?" Veronica asks.

"I mean the sound."

"I don't care," Ralph says. "If you two are getting it on. I'm just an old friend. If you two are getting it on, I'm happy for you. This kid is not my type, actually. I love her, but she's not my type. We spent the night together once, and it was a damp, damp evening. Many, many tears. You remember?"

"Don't remind me. I remember."

"The Brown Palace," Ralph says. "Denver's finest."

"You were trying very hard," Veronica says.

"I always try very hard. One of the nicest things about me. But you just sat there and wept, all night long. First I said to myself, Ralph, what is this? Is this a tactic? Is this a maneuver? If it's a tactic, what's the objective? I couldn't see an objective. So I decided it was grief, real grief."

"It was grief."

"So I said to myself, how am I to deal with this real, genuine grief? Room service? Booze? What?"

"Booze we already had."

"Stuff a cold, starve a fever," Ralph says. "I decided this was more in the cold area. We had their twenty-two dollar prime rib, if you remember."

"I had just busted up with Jack."

"So we're sitting there tearing up this twenty-two-dollar prime rib in the Brown Palace at four o'clock in the morning and she tells me I have a relentlessly pedestrian mind. Remember that?"

"I guess I was in a bad mood or something."

174

"I was not unaware of that," Ralph says. "Nevertheless it hurt me, at the time. Now I can laugh about it."

"I was probably too drunk to be as sensitive as I am when I'm not drunk," she says.

"You were pretty unhappy. You were probably thinking, what am I doing in this hotel room with this bozo?"

"I never thought of you that way. I always thought of you as kind of a friend."

"I just bought a new Mazda, gold in color," Ralph says. "People who are referred to as 'kind of a friend' tend to buy cars that are gold in color."

"Now you're feeling sorry for yourself," Veronica says. "Stop it."

"Back to Denver," Ralph says. "Denver and my gold Mazda."

"This round's on me," Simon says. "The same again? Everybody?"

IN the first dream he was grabbed by three or four cops for firing a chrome-plated .45 randomly in the street. He had no idea where he had gotten the .45 or why it was chrome-plated. In the second dream he awoke sitting on a lounge in a hotel lobby wearing pants and shoes but bare-chested. "I've got to find a shirt," he thought. Then he was in an apartment, which he recognized, trying to find a shirt. People were sleeping in the apartment and he kept banging into cymbals on stands placed here and there. He couldn't find a shirt. His mother came out of a closet and asked him to be a little quieter.

A sober conversation with Anne. "Tim asked Dore to come to work for Medlapse," she says. "He'll make

176

her a vice-president. To begin with, though, she'll have to be the secretary."

"It's got crash-and-burn written all over it."

"She'll be a vice-president."

"Like being vice-president of a bag of popcorn."

"I know," Anne says, sighing. "God I hate being a secretary. I did it for three years in Denver. These ass-holes telling you what to do."

"If you could do whatever you wanted—"

"I'd like to be an independent oil operator. There were a lot of those at home. Real party guys. Great hearts."

"Well," Simon says, "that's a skill too. You have to know how to con banks."

"I had one semester of geology."

"Maybe law school?"

"Terrible."

"You don't know that for a fact."

"I'm a total failure."

"Begin."

When the women began to get angry, Simon had not known quite how to react. They surprised him. He had, after all, done little more than give them a place to stay, feed them, sleep with them and talk to them, extending good Christian fellowship. But they had to be mad at somebody, he understood that, and even if they were mad at themselves still that was only starting the en-gine, as it were, the vehicle still had to go somewhere, win a race, explode, even. Veronica had come in one day with a headline from the *National Enquirer*,

177

BOY PRODUCES
100 YARDS OF
THREAD FROM
HIS RIGHT EYE

and said, "What can you do, Simon?"

Some days they were angry with him, some days they were angry with each other. Four people, many possibilities. Each person could be angry at any given point with one, two, or three others, or angry at the self. Two people could be angry at a third, three people at a fourth. He reached forty-nine possibilities before his math expired.

Their movement through the world required young men, a class to which he did not belong. Simon liked young men, within reasonable limits, and approved, in general, of the idea of young men and young women sleeping together in joyous disregard of history, economics, building codes. Let them have their four hundred square feet. Veronica liked garage apartments. Perhaps the young men would do well in the world, attend the new branch of Harvard Business in Gainesville, market a black bean soup that would rage through Miami like rabies or a voice attenuator capable of turning crackers into lisping Brits, and end up with seven thousand square feet in Paris on the Ile de la Cité. Young men had stiff pricks and smelled good, by and large, almost as good as babies. Young women bounced up and down on your chest and dazzled you with a thousand unexpected attacks. Simon counted the ways in which he was God-visited.

PARADISE

Sarah calls. "Do you know what she's done?" she
asks. She's referring to her mother.
"What?"
"Fallen in love."
Simon is astonished. "With whom?"
"The mayor. And he's married."
"Good God that's terrible."
"She was crying on my shoulder all last night."
"Oh Lord. Can I do anything?"
"Talk to her?"
"Would she want to talk to me about this?"
"I guess not. She said you were what she was trying
to get away from."
"I understand that. I understood that a long time
ago."
"Don't be bitter."
"Simple statement of fact. People get too much of
each other. Civility goes away, finally."
"Yeah I think you'd better butt out. Not that you've
had so much to do with the affairs of your Philadelphia
group lately."
"Well. Do you have enough money?"
"Daddy you've been asking me that since I was thir-
teen."
"It's a reflex. Listen, Sarah, is there anything I can do
for her, do you think? Or would it be better if I didn't
know about it?"
"I think she wants you to know about it. There's
nothing you can *do* about it."
"Is he in love with her?"

179

"He's a mayor. He needs a lot of love. More than other people. Oceans."

How does she know so much? "Keep me posted," he says.

"I dropped *Ways of Being, the East.*"

"Why?"

"It was boring and the guy lectured into his tie, mostly."

VERONICA'S trampoline is leaning against the wall and Veronica is throwing books at it to see how far they will bounce. *Buddenbrooks* in a paper edition bounces a good twelve feet. Dore is painting her legs red, with a two-inch brush and a big jar into which she has crumbled bright red Easter-egg glazes. Anne is threatening to cut off her long hair. She stands poised, a hank in one hand, scissors in the other, daring anyone to interfere. "Anybody messes with me gets the scissors in the medulla." Simon senses unrest.

A terrible night. Simon is in bed by ten, taking a Scotch for company. Anne and Dore are now watching television. Veronica is out somewhere. About ten-thirty Anne comes into the room, strips, and gets into bed with him.

"I'm chilly," she says.

He turns her on her stomach and begins to stroke her back, gently. A very sculptural waist, narrowing suddenly under the rib cage and then the hipbones flaring.

When Anne leaves to go back to her own bed, at two, Dore appears in the doorway.

"Are you all tired?" she asks.

"Probably." Dore climbs into the bed, clumsily, peels off her jeans and bikini pants, retaining the tank top which she's cut raggedly around the neck in the style of the moment. She takes his cock in hand and regards it thoughtfully.

"I'm sad and depressed," she says. "I feel useless. All I do is sit around and watch MTV."

"What do you want to do?"

"Something. But I don't know what."

"Lot of people in the same position," Simon says.

"I don't want to be a lawyer and I don't want to be a wife. I don't want to be a musician. What does that leave?"

"Be bad. Imagine something bad."

"Like what?"

"I have to tell you what to imagine?"

She looks at him. "There was this guy once. He asked me, are you a swallower or a spitter?"

"What'd you say?"

"He was a doctor. They tend to be crude."

He struggles around the bed and begins to kiss the insides of her thighs. "This is a terrible night."

"Why?"

182

"You guys aren't solving your problems. I can't help you very much." His hands are splayed out over her back, moving up and down, over the shoulders and down to the splendid buttocks. Thinking of buttercups and butterflies and flying buttresses and butts of malmsey.

"Veronica has a rash," she says, coming up for air.

"What kind of a rash?"

"Dark red. Looks like a wine stain."

"Where is it?"

"You'll see."

Saliva is running down his cock, token of enthusiasm.

Veronica walks in. "What is taking place here?" she asks, in a voice like thunder.

AFTER the women had departed Simon set up a small office in a barely renovated building on West Broadway. He was on the fourth floor, there was no air conditioning, and the big open windows brought in the clamor of the street, sirens, rape, outrage. His partners in Philadelphia sent him small jobs, much as one might UPS a fruitcake or a brace of pheasant to one recovering from an illness, with the implication that they were to be enjoyed not now but later, when he was stronger. He sat at his draughting table, a hollow-core door resting on carpenters' sawhorses, sketching on tracing paper with a felt pen. The problem was an office for a small foundation which had leased space in a very good block in the East Seventies. The difficulty

184

was that although there were floor-to-ceiling windows facing the street in the existing building, very little light reached the nether regions. He had designed a light scoop to be affixed to the rear of the building, but figured that the cost would be prohibitive. The fire escape was placed precisely where the tubing for the light scoop would have to go, and light scoops don't work very well anyhow, as both the tygers of wrath and the horses of instruction had taught him. Blake also had something to say about foundations:

Pity is become a trade, and generosity a science,
That men get rich by . . .

But that's a little hard, he thought, these people are doing the best they can, piloting worthy projects through the swamps of Inanition. To be working again felt very good.

SIMON thinks about Paradise. On the great throne, a naked young woman, her back to the viewer. Simon looks around for Onan, doesn't see him. Onan didn't make it to Paradise? Seems unfair. Great deal of marble about, he notices, shades of rose and terra-cotta; Paradise seems to have been designed by Edward Durell Stone. Science had worked out a way to cremate human remains, reduce the ashes to the size of a bouillon cube, and fire the product into space in a rocket, solving the Forest Lawn dilemma. Simon had once done a sketch problem on tomb sculpture, for his sophomore Visual Awareness course. No more tomb sculpture.

Paradise unearned. It was, rather, a gift, in this way

186

theologically unsound. It was a state or condition visited upon him, like being in the Army. Simon had walked around in green fatigues for most of two years, doing the best he could from day to day, sometimes carrying drunken comrades back to the barracks at night, outside Stuttgart, in a fireman's lift. His days were spent in meaningless maneuvers with giant weapons which the Army was afraid to fire for fear they wouldn't work. Mostly, when tested, they didn't. Simon read *Stars & Stripes* and very good mystery novels by John D. Macdonald. On leave in Berlin he tried to find buildings by Karl Friedrich Schinkel, whose work had not been lost on Mies. The women would soon be gone. The best thing he could do was to listen to them.

"I've had twenty-six years' practice in standing up. I can do it," Anne says.

She's wearing sweat pants with a dark gray crewneck sweater and medium-gray Reeboks. She's been drinking tequila and she's terribly drunk.

"I want to tell you something."

"What?"

"You think we're dumb bunnies."

"What makes you think that?"

"Your attitude."

Simon's been reading *Audubon Action*, "Arizona Dam Project Faces New Challenge."

"What's my attitude?"

"I see fatigue and disgust."

"Sweetie, that's not true."

"Don't call me sweetie."

"Anne," he says, "you want to sit down?"

"You think we're not bright enough for you."

"You're as bright as anybody. I mean it."

"You have an attitude of disdain. Sticks out all over you."

"Just not so."

"Veronica thinks you want us out."

"No. Untrue."

"She thinks your mind is wandering."

"That's what my mind does. Wander. Right now I'm thinking about the furniture of Paradise."

"What is it?"

"Knoll, basically." He pushes a sketch pad toward her. "But you see they haven't allowed for the angels who have only one wing, so I'm trying to—"

"The angels have only one wing?" she says in astonishment.

"Some angels have only one wing." He shows her an old engraving in which a single-winged angel is pictured.

"How can they fly with only one wing?"

"What makes you think they fly? In the literal sense?"

"I've always seen them with two wings."

"Artists like symmetry."

"He looks imperfect."

"You can get a lot accomplished with one wing. Fan the flames and lead the orchestra. I saw Buddy Rich, the drummer, play with a broken arm one night. Did more with one hand and his two feet than—"

188

"But it'd be like having only one breast." He slips a hand inside her shirt. Her breasts are bare. "If I'd spent the same amount of time worrying about my mind as I have worrying about my chest, I'd be Hegel by now," she says. "I mean since thirteen."

"Old Hegel."

"Don't be so snotty. We have Hegel in Denver."

"Hegel is quite sexy. Thesis, antithesis, synthesis."

"You think that's where he got the idea?"

"Could be."

Simon positions the white plaster egg eight feet tall in the sitting room. The women are watching. He smashes it with an iron-headed maul. Inside are three naked young men. Their names are Harry.

Q: I sometimes imagine that I am in Pest Control. I have a small white truck with a red diamond-shaped emblem on the door and a white jump suit with the same emblem on the breast pocket. I park the truck in front of a subscriber's neat three-hundred-thousand-dollar home, extract the silver canister of deadly pest-killer from the back of the truck, and walk up the brick sidewalk to the house's front door. Chimes ring, the door swings open, a young wife in jeans and a pink flannel shirt worn outside the jeans is standing there. "Pest Control," I say. She smiles at me, I smile back and move past her into the house, into the handsomely appointed kitchen. The canister is suspended by a sling from my right shoulder, and, pumping the mechanism occasionally with my right hand, I point the nozzle of

the hose at the baseboards and begin to spray. I spray
alongside the refrigerator, alongside the gas range,
under the sink, and behind the kitchen table. Next, I
move to the bathrooms, pumping and spraying. The
young wife is in another room, waiting for me to finish.
I walk into the main sitting room and spray discreetly
behind the largest pieces of furniture, an oak sideboard,
a red plush Victorian couch, and along the inside of the
fireplace. I do the study, spraying behind the master's
heavy desk on which there is an open copy of the *Co-
lumbia Encyclopedia,* he's been looking up the Seven
Years War, 1756-63, yellow highlighting there, and behind the forty-five-inch RCA television. The master
bedroom requires just touches, like perfume behind the
ear, short bursts in her closet which must avoid the two
dozen pairs of shoes there and in his closet which contains six to eight long guns in canvas cases. Finally I
spray the laundry room with its big white washer and
dryer, and behind the folding table stacked with sheets
and towels already folded. Who folds? I surmise that
she folds. Unless one of the older children, pressed into
service, folds. In my experience they are unlikely to
fold. Maybe the au pair. Finished, I tear a properly-
made-out receipt from my receipt book and present it
to the young wife. She scribbles her name in the appropriate space and hands it back to me. The house now
stinks quite palpably but I know and she knows that the
stench will dissipate in two to four hours. The young
wife escorts me to the door, and, in parting, pins a silver
medal on my chest and kisses me on both cheeks. Pest
Control!

FOUR o'clock in the morning. Simon listening to one of his radios, sipping white wine. Two horn players are talking about Coltrane.

"The thing is," one says, and the other bursts in to say, "Yeah, but wait a minute."

A Woody Shaw record is played. Simon's using earphones so he can play the music as loud as he pleases without disturbing the women. At low volume you lose half of it, a thing his wife had never understood. Now one of the guests is praising D flat. "This is on ITC," the host says. "ITC is a new label that's just getting started in LA. They're getting new guys and doing new things." The drummer on the Woody Shaw record is wonderfully skillful if a bit orotund.

"Great one," says one of the guys on the radio, when

the Wynton Marsalis track is over. "A lot of humility," says the other. "I mean he can do it all."

Simon suddenly remembers putting on his daughter's shoes, in the morning, before his wife took her to nursery school. His wife brought in the child and the shoes, and Sarah would sit on his lap as sneaker was fitted to foot. "Make your toes little," he'd say, and she'd perversely spread them.

"New York is a bitch," the radio says, "but there's more community."

Wheat-germ bubble gum was served
At the Maniacs' Ball

He lays himself down in bed, sleeps fitfully for an hour and a half. At six he's up again, in a t-shirt and jeans, moving around the apartment. The women are all still sleeping. He looks out of the windows. On the street a man in violet running shorts is carrying a woman on his shoulders, she's in fact riding him, her legs around his neck. The man is heavy, muscular, carries his rider with spectacular ease. The woman is in her early forties, the man the same age or a little younger. The man runs in circles, the woman waves like a circus performer. It's six-thirty.

When he goes out to get the *Times* there is a semi-corpse in the vestibule, a barely breathing Hispanic male. He's vomited blood and blood is all over the red tile. Simon shakes the man's shoulder. Whiskey smell and no visible wounds. He shakes the man again. No response.

There's a hospital at the end of the block. Simon, on

the sidewalk, stops a resident on the way to work. He's Oriental, Korean or Japanese, white-clothed, a stethoscope stuck in his right-hand jacket pocket.

"There's a man in here. Not in good shape."

The doctor looks annoyed.

"Call nine one one."

"I think you'd better look at him. He looks pretty far gone."

With clear reluctance the doctor, a small man with a mustache, follows Simon into the vestibule. He bends over the fallen man, taking care not to touch him.

"Call the hospital. Something in the—"

He moves one hand up and down his chest.

"Drunk, too."

Simon trudges back upstairs and telephones the hospital.

AND what if we grow old together, just the four of us? The loving quartet? What if we raddle together? They of course raddling at a rate less precipitant than my own. I have a quarter-century advantage, in terms of raddling. He's WAD, as the medical students say, Whirling Around the Drain. What kind of old ladies will these old ladies be? Veronica will be, as ever, moody. She'll do something immensely foolish, like writing a book. The book will be an extended meditation on the word "or," or the road not taken, or the road taken but not enjoyed, or the road taken and enjoyed to the fullest, a celebration of "or" not less funsome than Kierkegaard's. Twelve people will read the book. Four will write her letters. I will read the book but not write her a letter. "Good work," I will say to Veronica, clapping her on the shoulder several times to signal hearty congratulation. "That type . . ." The book will have been set in Bulmer, a typeface most eloquent, anorexic Bodoni but speaking nevertheless. Veronica will bring me my toddy as I sit by the fire, two pints of tequila laced with capers and a little gunpowder. She'll kiss my knee, which will probably, by this time, resemble a drill bit. I'll place my claw in her hair, now red and a very convincing red thanks to improved Dupont manipulation of the Periodic Table. The old folks at home.

Dore will come in and demand to know where my penis has got to. I don't know, I'll say, it was there yesterday, more or less. You call that *there*, she'll say, scornfully, and I'll say, I am a poor relic, a poor husk, a leftover, a single yellow bean covered with Cling Wrap sailing on a flawed plate through the refrigerator of life. Yes, she'll say, excuses, you promised us Eden, you did, I remember, not anything you said in so many words but by implication, you implied that we would be happy forever together . . . I didn't! I'll say, or scream, I always said that things would turn out badly, consult the records, look at the transcript, you have no right to—

Anne

"It's the fault of men. As a group."

"They don't want us to bloom and flower."

"Trying to keep all the prosperity for a few self-selected individuals. Men."

"I've endured it on every side."

"Whole societies have taken glee and satisfaction from heckling, humiliating and scourging me."

"Thought I heard a skunk barking."

"They are tearing me apart with their defamations that whole worlds chuckle about."

"I think we should buy some cars or something, Firebirds and Cutlasses."

"The inconsequence of your thought is a burden to me."

197

"Stick a screwdriver down your throat if you mess with me. A big screwdriver."

"Gotta get that bird's nest on the ground."

"You can start, in America, with just a nickel, and pretty soon you have a dime!"

"I've been busy, sorting buttons, one thing and another."

"Polishing the doorknobs and getting the fug out of the corners."

"A few rows of figgers I'd like you to check over."

"Used to be able to stay up all night and roar. Can't do that now."

"Wash my fingers frequently, bubbling in responses to forms and questionnaires."

"We watched a movie in which a giant chandelier visited the earth and a lot of little green wimps hung about the edges of the frame, cooing."

"Yeah I saw that one."

"Guy came up to me on the street, black guy, he says, 'Can you spare a quarter for an American citizen?' "

"You gave it to him."

"How could I not?"

"Caught in the cognitive squeeze."

"Pink always struck me as sordid."

"He's got those little spots on his hands."

"Burns. From cooking fried chicken. The grease jumps."

"If men knew what they were doing, they would cringe with fear."

198

PARADISE

"Older people should be treated with respect, not much but some."

"That's really a very fine attitude toward older people. I admire you for that."

"It's hard to be bright and fresh when you're too old."

"You can accidentally shoot your dog. I've known cases of that."

"Old men with canes gimping down the sidewalk. White hair and bent heads."

"I dreamed about this pony last night. Very engaging pony. We kept it in Simon's room."

"They found more rabid skunks. Two in Brooklyn Heights and one at the World Trade Center."

"If they get here, how will they get here?"

"From Brooklyn, they have to walk over the bridge. From downtown, all they have to do is walk up Hudson Street."

"They could be on Hudson Street already. We wouldn't know."

"They could be in the graveyards. Hiding out in the graveyards behind the sagging stones. We wouldn't know."

"If they bite you then you're dead."

"No you have to have shots in the stomach. Forty-two shots in the stomach."

"What they do is bite your domestic animals, your cats and dogs, and then your domestic animals bite you. Or they bite other domestic animals and eventually somebody bites you. Or your children."

199

"I'm going to stay off the streets."

"No just wear boots. Then if one approaches you you can kick it."

"What does a skunk look like? I've never seen one."

"It looks like a wallaby except that it has a different kind of head. Less attenuated. They're black."

"I've only seen them squashed on the road."

"Maybe we should put chicken wire over the windows."

"I think we're getting into a panic here. Just wear boots."

"Let Simon deal with them."

"Do you think he's brave?"

"No I don't think he's brave. But I think he's smart."

"If he's smart why doesn't he make us happy?"

"Who can make us happy? I mean if you look at it realistically."

"He said his wife finally asked him to stop introducing her to people as 'my wife.'"

"That's not unreasonable."

"One day there won't be any wives any more."

"Or husbands either."

"Just free units cruising the surface of the earth. Flying the black flag."

"Something to look forward to."

"Do you really think so?"

"What about the children?"

"Get one and keep it. Keep it for yourself. Hug it and teach it things. Everything you know."

"But they need fathers, in theory. That kind of quality, that kind of rough quality . . . "

"I forgot about boys."

"Reminds me of thick lumber stacked on the back of a truck, held down by chains—"

"How can we leave him?"

"How can we not leave him?"

"He's gracious and good."

"He's not the only pebble on the beach."

"It's an impossible situation."

"But I like it."

"The thing is, whether we believe in ourselves or not."

"It's like three people reading a magazine at the same time."

"But we'll never see him again."

"We'll send postcards."

"Little satisfaction in that."

"Well you can't have everything."

"Something is better than nothing."

"The thing is, we just have to have the courage of our convictions."

"Well I've learned this: To make progress, you have to give up something."

"How do you know that's true?"

"It sounds right. It includes pain."

"I have hope," Simon says. "Not a hell of a lot of hope, but some hope. You need tons of hope simply in order to function. Got to think that everything will work out. I don't think that's condescending. I hope it's not condescending. I've dealt with young people before. I taught Sarah to roll her eyes and groan, when she was four, we rehearsed it. She was attempting it already, herself, but she hadn't got it right. My father believed in the Second World War, a good choice. I believe in bricklayers but even bricklayers get things wrong, you specify a course of contrasting brick, vary the pattern of headers and stretchers and they misread the blueprints. I don't want to be condescending. Trees have integrity, can't go far wrong with a tree. You want

202

to make a building look good, budget heavily for trees. A bird in the tree is better than a kick in the prosthesis. That's all I mean. Thank you and good night."

"Simon, I don't want to go," Anne says.

"I don't want you to go."

"But I have to."

"I understand that. But you could be foolish and unwise."

"You'd get tired of me."

"No. The reverse, if anything. We could sit around and watch old movies on television. That's all I ask."

"That's not true."

"I ask you, formally, to stay. Will you stay?"

"No."

"Why not?"

"It wouldn't work out."

"We could enjoy it for a short time. Might be as much as two whole years."

"You make it sound like a cancer situation. It wouldn't be fair to the others."

"When is anything ever fair to the others?"

SIMON flew to North Carolina to inspect a job he'd done in Winston-Salem, a hospital. The construction was quite good and he found little to complain of. He admired the fenestration, done by his own hand. He spent an agreeable night in a Ramada Inn and flew back the next day. His seatmate was a young German woman on her way to Frankfurt. She was six months pregnant, she said, and her husband, an Army sergeant in Chemical Warfare, had found a new girl friend, was divorcing her. She had spent two years at Benning, loved America, spoke with what seemed to Simon a Texas accent. Her father was dead and her mother operated a candy store in Frankfurt. They talked about pregnancy and delivery, about how much wine she allowed herself, whether aspirin was in fact a danger to the baby, and how both of her brothers-in-law had been born in taxis. She was amazingly cheerful given the circumstances and told him that the Russians were probably going to attempt to take over Mexico next. We had neglected Mexico, she said.

Over the Atlantic on the long approach to Kennedy Simon saw a hundred miles of garbage in the water, from the air white floating scruff. The water became agitated at points as fish attacked the garbage and Simon turned his mind to compaction. When they landed he kissed the German woman goodbye and told her that although she probably didn't feel very lucky at the moment, she was very lucky.

"I got to go away now," Dore says. "I got to leave this place."

"I gots to make mah mark in de whirl," says Veronica.

"The prophet Zephaniah appeared to me in a dream," Anne says. "He said, Split! Split!"

"Time boogies on," Dore says.

They are gathered by the door with much duffel. Aspects of optimistic gloom.

" 'Bye guys," Simon says.

They lurch through the door.

Q: Maybe they'll come back.

A: No, no. Of course not. Why should they?

Q: Do you want them to come back?

A: I have peculiar dreams. But I sleep very well, on balance.

Q: How many hours a night?

A: Four or five.

Q: Some people like Giacometti. As a sculptor. Although I suppose it's foolish to speak of "liking" Giacometti. Armature with impetigo. He's not about women.

A: Yes he is. Also, he's got a razor in his shoe.

Q: Do you want some of these little green ones? They're supposed to be good.

207

Donald Barthelme

A: I think not.
Q: Feels like Saturday today, I don't know why . . .
A: It does feel a bit like Saturday . . .

PARADISE

Simon, a fifty-three-year-old Philadelphia architect, has been given an almost miraculous gift—a year of his own, to do with as he wishes. In a large, bare New York apartment, he lives like a ghost, thinking back on an unsuccessful marriage and his working life. Through a combination of circumstances he becomes involved with three young and beautiful women, who come to live with him. He is twice as old as they are, as they cheerfully and repeatedly point out, yet is drawn into a shifting, complex relationship. The three women, Dore, Veronica, and Anne, are very different, lively and intelligent but in important ways lost in the world, grappling for purchase. For the eight months of their stay, alternately advancing and retreating, they test the possibilities of the liaison, as Simon, from the special perspective of one not young, awaits their inevitable departure.

This spare, deliberate novel, at once horrifically comic and bluntly melan-